STEAM
RAILWAYS
EXPLAINED

Steam, Oil & Locomotion

STAN YORKE

D0273214

First published 2007
© Stan Yorke, 2007

COUNTRYSIDE BOOKS
3 Catherine Road
Newbury, Berkshire

To view our complete range of books,
please visit us at
www.countrysidebooks.co.uk

ISBN 978 1 84674 012 1

Photographs by the author
Illustrations by Trevor Yorke

Designed by Peter Davies, Nautilus Design
Produced through MRM Associates Ltd., Reading
Typeset by CJWT Solutions, St Helens
Printed by Borcombe Printers plc, Romsey

CONTENTS

Acknowledgements

✦

The writing of a book such as this calls upon the knowledge of a great number of people, such is the diversity of the various components that make up our railways. I would like to place on record my thanks to the dozens of volunteers and employees of the various preserved railways who answered endless questions with both patience and enthusiasm. I have listed below those railways that feature along with their picture caption abbreviations.

Bluebell Railway	(BR)
Bodmin and Wenford Railway	(BWR)
Buckinghamshire Railway Centre	(BRC)
Chinnor and Princes Risborough Railway	(CPRR)
Churnet Valley Railway	(CVR)
Crich Tramway Village	(CTV)
Dartmoor Railway	(DR)
Dean Forest Railway	(DFR)
Didcot Railway Centre	(DRC)
East Lancashire Railway	(ELR)
Embsay and Bolton Abbey Steam Railway	(EBASR)
Gloucestershire Warwickshire Railway	(GWR)
Great Central Railway	(GCR)
Keighley and Worth Valley Railway	(KWVR)
Kent and East Sussex Railway	(KESR)
Lavender Line	(LL)
Llangollen Railway	(LR)
Mid Hants Railway	(MHR)
Midland Railway – Butterley	(MR)
The Museum of Science and Industry	(MSI)
National Railway Museum – York	(NRMY)
National Railway Museum – Shildon	(NRMS)
Nene Valley Railway	(NVR)
North Yorkshire Moors Railway	(NYMR)
Paignton and Dartmouth Steam Railway	(PDSR)
Peak Rail	(PR)
Severn Valley Railway	(SVR)
South Devon Railway	(SDR)
Swanage Railway	(SR)
Welsh Highland Railway	(WHR)
West Somerset Railway	(WSR)

Introduction

The word 'railway' probably conjures up some of the widest ranges of images and emotions known to man. To some, it's a memory of far-off sunny holidays, of adventure and exploration; to many, it is sadly a daily fight with crowds and bad timekeeping. Yet, for most of us, the railways and, in particular, steam engines, will always hold a fascination.

Having waded through dozens of railway books it seems, though, as with so many industrial subjects, you have to choose between children's books or deep, detailed tomes which hardly constitute easy reading. This book has been written in an attempt to bridge that gap. As with all the *Explained* series, the idea is to go beyond the characters involved in a part of our history, to look at how the subject worked, and how and why it was created. This knowledge will hopefully engender greater pleasure when visiting today's lovingly restored railways and indeed may even lighten the frustration

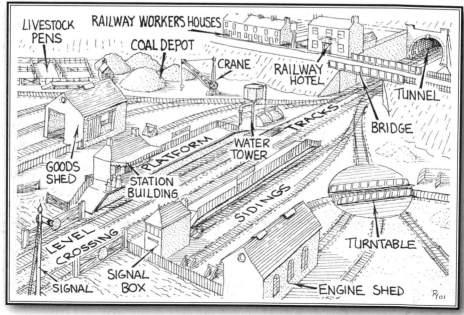

General overview of the common features of railways.

of sitting in a stationary train at eight o'clock in the morning!

The book is split into four sections. In Section I we take a brief journey back in time to see the origins of our railway system. Here we meet such names as Stephenson and Brunel, and get a glimpse of the effects the early railways had on our society. Sections II and III consider in detail the way the railways were built and run – the main 'explaining' part of the book. We look at all the static items like the track and the stations before, in Section III, we get to the engines and the rolling stock. It is difficult to resist running straight into the engines as they represent the core image of earlier railways but, as I hope you will discover, so much else is essential before a train can actually move.

Section IV describes the scene today, in particular, the twenty or so restored and working steam railways that exist around our country. At this juncture I must put in a word of warning. The railways have a very complicated history featuring a great number of developments and inventions. For every example I give there are bound to be different versions, depending on the region or the designer. This is particularly so when looking at engines, which engender passionate loyalty in enthusiasts. In a modest book like this the author obviously has to take considerable liberties and omit vast amounts of detail. As always, I have tried to avoid long-winded and over-technical terms – this is a book to ignite your interest in railways, not a manual on becoming a railway engineer!

Stan Yorke

Steam, hot oil and hard work. Preparing two restored GWR locomotives for a day's work on the Severn Valley Railway.

SECTION I

A
BRIEF
HISTORY

CHAPTER I

In The Beginning

Like so many aspects of the Industrial Revolution, our railways developed surprisingly slowly. Man had long realised that the wheel enables heavy loads to be moved easily; he had also observed that the smoother the roadway the easier was the task. In England this knowledge was applied some time in the 1600s by laying down flat wooden planks secured to stone blocks set into the ground. A wooden peg fitted to the wagon would run between the 'rails' acting as the guide. These early wooden tracks were used only for wagons pushed by men. Soon wagonways using oak rails, some 4 inches square, pinned to stones set in ballast, became standard. Wagons carrying about 30 cwt were used, each being pulled by a horse. These rails only lasted about a year and to combat the wear the top surface was covered by a

FIG 1.1: *Typical early wooden wagon with cast wheels and flanges. This restored wagon from the Stratford and Moreton Railway is standing on a section of the original cast iron fish-belly track. Opened in 1826, this horse-drawn line worked for some 60 years.*

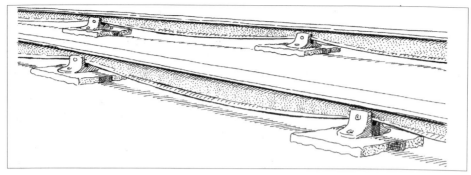

FIG 1.2: *Sketch of fish-belly track.*

cast iron plate. In this form these wagonways spread all over the country, moving coal and stones down to the nearest navigable water and carrying ever heavier loads.

It seems that from very early on in England the guiding peg was replaced by wheels that had flanges which kept the wagon on the rails. As iron became more available, cast iron 'edge' rails were made, usually only around 3 ft in length, with the joints supported by a sleeper or stone block. To give greater strength, the central, unsupported area was made deeper in what were known as fish-bellied rail. By the 1820s, wrought iron rail was being made in 15 ft (4.5m) lengths but, as these rails were rolled from red-hot iron, rather than cast into a mould, it was not easy to alter the cross-section; so the fish-belly shape was abandoned and instead

FIG 1.3: *L-shaped tram plateway, showing how the plain wheels had to run over any stones or debris.*

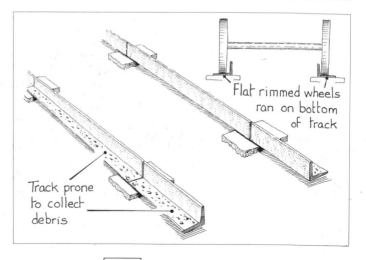

Flat rimmed wheels ran on bottom of track

Track prone to collect debris

more sleepers or stone blocks were used. The rail was held in a chair by wooden wedges, a system that lasted until the Second World War. An alternative rail was also developed, sometimes referred to as tram plateway. This rail was L-shaped and again held to stone blocks. The wagon wheels, without any flanges, now ran on the bottom of the rail and possibly because they appeared simpler and needed less precision, these plateways spread very fast. By the 1820s, though, the plateways were seen as less sturdy and prone to clogging up with dirt and loose stones and the edge rail became standard for new works, though some horse-drawn plateways lasted into the 20th century.

The wheels, originally all wood, were soon being made with iron rims, which greatly extended their life and, by the 1820s, the whole wheel was cast from iron.

The steam engine had been developed in the early 1700s but these first examples were, strictly speaking, atmospheric engines. Their power came from developing a partial vacuum and allowing the natural atmospheric

FIG 1.4: *A working reconstruction of Richard Trevithick's Pen-Y-Darren locomotive on display in the Ironbridge Gorge Museum. The driver worked at the left-hand end whilst the fireman rode on a separate 'tender' on the right.*

pressure to provide the power stroke. Using steam at pressures above a few pounds per square inch (psi) was thought to be very dangerous; indeed, with the early ironwork this was partially true. By the end of the 18th century, though, men like Richard Trevithick were experimenting with true steam engines, which used the steam pressure to push a piston inside a cylinder. His first machines were steam-driven road vehicles but, no matter how he tried, the roads of the day simply were not good enough to support the heavy machines. Samuel Homfray owned an ironworks in Pen-y-Darren in South Wales and had bought a share in Trevithick's patents; he also had a 9-mile plateway down to the Glamorganshire Canal. Thus, the world's first steam locomotive was born, moving a 10-ton load without trouble, but alas its weight proved too much for the cast iron plateway, which frequently broke. A second locomotive was tried on the wagonway of the Wylem colliery near Newcastle upon Tyne but, though it was able to do the job, its weight again proved too much for the crude track.

Meanwhile, the road system was being improved and turnpike roads, where the tolls paid for the improvements, were spreading, as were the coaching services. The problem, however, was the vast increase in the need for goods transport created during the early part of the Industrial Revolution, in particular for coal, which was way beyond the capacity of the roads and canals.

During the early years of the 19th century two rather odd railways had opened: the Surrey Iron Railway in 1803 and the delightful Oystermouth and Swansea Railway in 1804. The former ran from Wandsworth to Croydon, some 8¼ miles, and was later extended to Merstham, a further 8½ miles. The track was tram plateway, set at a gauge of 4 ft 2 inches, and was almost flat to Croydon, which allowed a single horse to pull five or six wagons each carrying some 3 tons. This was the world's first public railway. The Swansea line, again horse-drawn, was built to carry stone from a nearby quarry but soon changed to a passenger line. Extended to Mumbles in 1900 after a very chequered career, it continued to carry passengers right up to its closure in 1960. It can claim to have been the world's first passenger-carrying railway.

A turning point came in 1818 when a decision was made to build a railway rather than a canal to improve the movement of coal from the South Durham coalfields to the River Tees. The line was to run from Stockton to Darlington and included two inclines, where the wagons would be hauled up and down using a stationary engine and ropes. Opened in 1825, the line used both horses and steam locomotives, though only horses were trusted to pull passenger coaches. Steam engines were still very unreliable and, though due to operating errors rather than their construction, two engines exploded in 1828. Nevertheless, more mines adopted the steam locomotive to move their coal, particularly around Newcastle.

Across the Pennines in Lancashire another revolution was taking place in the cotton trades. Manchester was growing at an alarming rate, as was its insatiable demand for raw cotton imported through Liverpool, plus coal for its factories. Manchester had doubled in size between 1800 and 1825 and, during the same period, Liverpool's docks had seen the number of ships using the port more than double.

The full story of the early transport links between Liverpool and Manchester would fill a large book, but suffice to say it involved greed and overcharging. It was in the 1820s that the frustrated industrialists turned their backs on the canal and river companies and determined to build a railway. The engineers had learnt a great deal from building canals over the previous 50 years, but so had the landowners, who now realised how to manipulate Parliament to their advantage. Fired by a mixture of rumour and mis-

FIG 1.5: *A working replica of Stephenson's Rocket built in 1979, normally on show in the National Railway Museum York but, as here, often on tour around other preserved railways. (BRC)*

information, many people protested at the very idea of a railway, often using violence against the surveyors. The problem was further complicated by the fact that the great centres of enterprise, like Birmingham, Manchester and Liverpool, were run by go-ahead Quaker families who were barred from becoming Members of Parliament. This lack of direct representation weakened the passage of railway bills through Parliament for many years. The physical effects of these difficulties can still be seen today in the strange routes taken by some of the early railways, apparently ignoring sizeable towns, but this was usually because of the high jinks of the local landowners and MPs.

The Liverpool and Manchester Railway was surveyed three times, firstly in 1822 by William James, assisted by a bright young student from Edinburgh College by the name of Robert Stephenson. The second survey, two years later, was carried out by George Stephenson, Robert's father, but again the Bill failed due to his lack of experience in dealing with parliamentary committees. Finally, under the watchful eye of John Rennie, a third survey by Charles Vignoles was carried out and, in 1826, the Bill was finally passed. Four years of formidable

FIG 1.6: *Another working replica, this time of Stephenson's locomotive* Planet. *The original was built in 1830, soon after* Rocket, *and shows just how fast progress was made in the early days of engine building. On show in the Manchester Museum of Science & Technology.*

construction followed before the line was ready. Gone were the old flanged plateways; the Liverpool and Manchester would use wrought iron edge rails – the wheel running on top of the rail as we are used to today. The directors, however, were still divided between stationary engines hauling the trains by ropes, or steam locomotives. Following a protest from George Stephenson they chose locomotives but, to ensure they got the best, they instigated a competition to be held on the new line at Rainhill. Though several of the entries had excellent features, Robert Stephenson's engine *Rocket* won the day and soon the trains were running. Driven by the need to move goods, the company was surprised at the passenger traffic that developed. A dividend was paid at the end of the first year and just as the Bridgewater Canal had heralded the start of the canal era, so the Liverpool and Manchester Railway sealed the role of railways for decades to come.

The early 1830s saw many more key lines open, as London was linked to Birmingham, Bristol and Southampton. The growth was quite extraordinary, as a few figures will quickly show. Just fifteen years later, in the 'railway mania' year of 1845, some 620 different lines were proposed, with yet more waiting their turn the following year. By now all the sensible routes had long been built and these later lines were barely viable and many people lost great amounts of invested money. By 1840, over 4,000 route miles had been built and, by 1847, some 45,000 people were employed by the railway companies.

Another rather odd provision was becoming of concern to the railways – time. In the early 1800s each town still set its clocks to the 'true' time as shown by a sundial. Thus, Plymouth was some twenty minutes behind London – of no importance to the good people of Devon but a problem to the railway, which had to organise its trains by time. Slowly the railways introduced London time as the basis of the timetables, particularly for the east–west routes. At first this was referred to as 'railway time' but, as the idea was taken up by more companies, London (or Greenwich) time became standard throughout the land.

By the 1850s, many of the smaller companies were being bought out by the larger, usually older, companies with names that would last until the massive reorganisation of 1923. All these larger companies had engineering works where they built their own engines, wagons and coaches. Towns like Swindon, Crewe, Derby and Doncaster expanded to serve the railways. Rivalry was passionate and the pride can still be seen if we just consider some of the rival London termini: Paddington – the Great Western Railway; Marylebone – the Great Central Railway; Euston – the London and North Western Railway; St Pancras – the Midland Railway; King's Cross – the Great Northern Railway; Liverpool Street – the Great Eastern Railway; Cannon Street and Charing Cross – the South Eastern and Chatham Railways; Waterloo – the London and South Western Railway; Victoria – the London, Brighton and

South Coast Railway. Several of these were shared between two companies but it illustrates the need to have a presence in the capital. There was never a 'London' station used by every company, the railways were born of local enterprise and stayed local to the end.

By now, the locomotive had developed to a shape we would easily recognise and even the coaches were losing their stagecoach appearance. One oddity remained: the GWR under Brunel had adopted a track gauge of 7 ft (2.13m) rather than the standard 4 ft 8½ inches (1.43m). This was

FIG 1.7: *Brunel's oddity, the 7 ft broad gauge system. A working replica of the 1840 broad gauge loco* Fire Fly, *seen here running on mixed gauge track at the Didcot Steam Centre.*

FIG 1.8: *Preserved railways aren't all steam, as this restored 1956 British Railways-built diesel unit shows. (MR)*

technically superior but made transfer of goods between the GWR and the rest of the system a time-consuming problem; so, reluctantly, the GWR started to lay dual gauge track and eventually (1892) all the broad gauge running stopped. Alas, not a single broad gauge engine has survived from this era. Brunel had also tried out a completely different form of power on the South Devon line between Exeter and Newton Abbot, in which there was no engine on the train at all. He erected a large pipe between the rails into which a piston ran, drawn by the vacuum created in the pipe by stationary engines at the side of the line. The train was connected to the piston, which dragged the train along. This link passed through a slot in the top of the pipe, which was sealed by a leather flap. This was one of three atmospheric lines built but leakage was always a problem and the experiment was ended after just one year.

FIG 1.9:
Sketch showing how the train was pulled by the piston in the pipe. In practice the unit was fitted to a small wagon on which the hapless driver sat.

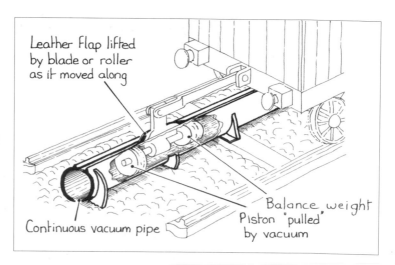

Leather flap lifted by blade or roller as it moved along

Continuous vacuum pipe

Piston 'pulled' by vacuum

Balance weight

FIG 1.10: *Possibly the sole surviving section of Brunel's South Devon vacuum railway pipework. The 15 ins diameter cast iron tube was laid between broad gauge rails – the leather flap along the top has long since rotted away. (DRC)*

CHAPTER 2

The Glorious Years

O ne important event was to occur in the mid 19th century, the arrival of cheap steel. Steel had been made in small quantities for centuries but its high cost limited it to articles like swords and armour. Steel is made from iron by carefully adjusting the carbon content, plus the addition of a small percentage of other chemicals, each combination giving rise to a different type of steel. After many attempts, the mass conversion of cheap, cast iron into steel was made practical by Henry Bessemer and his converter, heralding its widespread availability. Steel is ideal for rails and it revolutionised the manufacture of engines, wheels, springs and axles, resulting in a dramatic rise in the speed and comfort of rail travel.

Each company still produced its own locomotives, coaches and wagons, all decorated in the company's own livery – these must have been very colourful times. In the 1850s, over 70 million passengers were being carried each year, plus vast amounts of goods. The roads may well have improved but longer road journeys were still slow and uncomfortable. The canal system also began to give up the unequal struggle and many were sold to the railway companies, who either closed down their old rivals or used them to provide a feeder service to the railways.

Though not the subject of this book we must also recognise that railways had spread to every continent. We may have started it, indeed we exported vast amounts of rail and locomotives but, alas, today we import nearly all of our railway needs.

FIG 2.1: *Two examples of company crests. On the left, the South Eastern & Chatham Railway, on the right, the Metropolitan Railway.*

Apart from locomotive works built by the railway companies, there were other independent companies who not only built for the home railways but produced most of the exported machines.

Various special trains had evolved: even Queen Victoria travelled in the first Royal Train of dedicated coaches. Coaches and wagons had been designed for an enormous range of requirements. One could pay for a family coach, set out with areas for the family, the luggage and the servants, which could then be transferred from one company to another to enable a through journey to be completed without any interruption for the traveller. Enormous coal trains moved up to 1,000 tons at a time from South Wales and the Durham coalfields, using special engines designed just for this traffic. The logistics required by all this employed an army of administration staff, including the Railway Clearing House, which organised the appropriate division of fares when a journey involved more than one company.

The lot of the long-suffering passengers also improved, as coaches

FIG 2.2: *The most powerful locomotive ever built in the UK, one of over 100 such engines built by the North British Locomotive Company of Glasgow in 1953 for the South African Railways. The climax of over a century of exporting locomotives to every corner of the world. (BRC)*

became longer and more comfortable. The Pullman Company was supplying the ultimate in luxury, though only for use on just a few top-named trains. Originally there had been three classes of passenger – First, Second and Third – and a train would either be all first class or all second and third. By the end of the 19th century, second class was abolished and all trains carried first and third class accommodation, just as they still do, though the slightly derogatory 'third' has now become 'standard'. Most coaches were still made of separate compartments, each seating up to ten passengers, but corridor coaches were starting to appear on mainline trains. These offered toilet and dining facilities – at last trains could travel long distances without having to make comfort stops! The emergency cord had also become standard. There were now over 18,000 miles of track and the passenger figures exceeded 3 million per day.

This might be a good point at which to reflect that all inland transport for some 60 years, between 1830 and 1890, was pulled either by a horse or a steam locomotive. We have to imagine a world with no universally available electricity, no cars or lorries, no air travel. Yet this period was the zenith of the British Empire.

Another familiar cry was also widespread – complaints about timekeeping! *The Times* commented in 1900: 'the marvel is, not that some

FIG 2.3: *A pair of beautifully restored coaches dating from 1911, designed for the Great Western Railway by G. H. Churchward. (SVR)*

FIG 2.4: *A rare survivor from the past, a class 0298 well tank, built in 1874 for the London and South Western Railway. Three survived into the 1960s, working in Cornwall, and two of these have now been fully restored. (BRC)*

FIG 2.5: *An early four-wheeled coach which survived to be restored, having been used as a camping coach. (SDR)*

FIG 2.6: *Four interior shots of the coaches in Fig 2.3. Each compartment had numbered seats, with overhead baggage racks, plus the inevitable pictures of places served by the railway. Each had its own sliding door onto the corridor, plus its own outer door with adjustable window on the other side, and in the corridor ran the new emergency cord with dire warnings for improper use!*

trains are late, but that any trains ever run to time at all'.

The last main line, the Great Central, was built with romantic hopes of a Channel tunnel and continental traffic.

The tunnel had, in fact, been started, and trial borings made at the end of the 1870s had reached nearly a mile, but the British military thought it might be a serious threat to our security and the work stopped. This was the only line to be built in Britain with the slightly larger clearances used on the continent. Several main lines received improvements that bypassed busy cities to enable fast, long-distance trains to be run. The greatest increase in line mileage, though, came from the local branch line. In 1896, legislation had introduced the 'light railway'; limited in both weight and speed, it permitted a much cheaper construction. This was the era of romantic, twisting local lines, run in a slightly ramshackle way.

At the same time, however, the seeds of great change were already being sown. Werner von Siemens had demonstrated a miniature electric locomotive, hauling passengers at the Crystal Palace in 1881 and, in 1883, street trams had been built. In Germany, Rudolf Diesel had invented the diesel engine around 1897. In 1902, on the London and South West lines, automatic electrically-controlled pneumatic signals were being installed. In 1903, the Mersey Railway had been electrified, followed by the Lancashire and Yorkshire company's lines between

FIG 2.7: *Resplendent in LNER apple green, Doncaster-built V2 class* Green Arrow *awaits departure from Loughborough station. Typical of Gresley's fine three-cylinder locomotives designed and built in the 1920s. (GCR)*

Liverpool and Southport. Between 1909 and 1912, lines south of London were being electrified and eventually these covered most of the Southern Region's suburban lines, though this was partly in response to losing commuter traffic to the electric street trams.

The First World War took a terrible toll on the railway system. Robbed of investment and heavily used, it emerged in a very sad state. Something had to be done and the result was the official 1923 grouping, in which almost all the railway companies were amalgamated into just four large companies – the Southern (SR), the Great Western (GWR), the London, Midland and Scottish (LMS), and the London and North Eastern (LNER). Though this is always spoken of as the '1923 grouping', it had, in fact, been done as part of the war effort in 1914. In 1923, it was simply given formal, legal status. Whilst great internal battles ensued as to who was going to be in charge of what, the change out in the real world was slow but steady. New liveries and

FIG 2.8: *Electric street trams were used in several large cities and prompted many railway companies to review their suburban services. This is a restored Glasgow tram, built in 1922. (CTV)*

FIG 2.9: *The height of luxury travel. There are several relatively modern Pullman coaches restored and in use today. (KESR)*

company colours started to appear, along with better long distance services that crossed old company borders, and there was less paperwork.

Partly driven by the need for ever longer trains, but spiced up by the competition between companies that served the same areas, the post-grouping era saw the peak of steam locomotive design, many examples of which are thankfully still with us, even if extensively rebuilt. For instance, it was possible to travel from London to Exeter, Plymouth and the West Country via two competing routes. The same was true for the London to Birmingham route and most famously, London to Scotland. This latter service saw the so-called Great North Races between the Euston, Crewe route (LMS) and the rival King's Cross, York route (LNER). The crack trains ran with fewer coaches and were given top priority to keep going at all costs. Holiday trains now grew to enormous lengths and 16 or 18-coach trains were not uncommon, though to be fair the coaches were not quite as long as now. Mainline trains were averaging 70 mph and indeed many services from this period were faster than we manage today. By the 1930s, the Midland Railway had commissioned two mainline diesel locomotives and diesel shunters were common. Pioneered by the GWR, diesel railcars and diesel multiple units (DMUs) started to take over rural lines.

The Second World War again punished the railway system heavily, everything being maintained on a 'just enough to keep it running' basis. The track was poor, the engines dirty and worn out. Yet again, something had to be done and the politicians, true to form, decided on a regrouping. This time, though, everything was to go into one large state-controlled pot, British Railways. The repairs were done, a whole new range of standard, easy to service, steam locomotives were designed, but the glorious days were gone forever. More people now had their own cars. Lorries and the new motorways took more and more of the traffic and then, with what to many seemed indecent haste, the end of steam was announced. Diesel engines took over most mainline services and, while not very romantic, they made a good job of it and saved a great deal of dirty work. Engine depots, needed to service steam engines with coal and water, cleaning the fires and disposing of the ash, and turning them around virtually every day, disappeared. Diesels, like electric engines, just started up and went. By 1966, it was all over and gone. The infamous Dr Beeching had been given the task of analysing the railway, for the first time incidentally, and his report showed that vast parts of

FIG 2.10: *GWR Railcar number 22 built in 1940 and now fully restored once more. These were the precursors of our modern diesel units which still ply the smaller branch lines on their own. (DRC)*

FIG 2.11: *The Southern Railway developed a vast network of electrified lines in the 1920s, using electric light signals and a 600 V DC third rail system, still in use today. This view from Horsham station shows a twelve-coach train setting off south. The SR had always used the system of long trains from London which slowly split up as they moved into the country. This monster will split between Bognor Regis and Portsmouth.*

FIG 2.12: *The 3,300 hp English Electric-built Deltic diesel locomotives took over the East Coast main line services and became famous for their long life and service. Many completed over 3 million miles before being retired in 1981. (NRM)*

the system ran at a loss – thus departed the rural lines. The worst part of this process wasn't the motive to be efficient, but the way in which lines were made to look as bad as possible. Passenger figures, for instance, were taken during track workdays when buses were providing a substitute service. Every device was used to disparage them and nowhere was there talk of streamlining these local services to make them more efficient. Again, to be fair, Beeching also recommended in a second report more investment in the viable main line services.

Whilst all this post-war change was taking place, small bands of people were taking a rather different approach. Often accused of being anti-progress, they thought that we shouldn't rip up and fill in everything that wasn't modern. They wanted a viable link to our glorious past, a living reminder of how we had reached the second half of the 20th century. Thus was born that peculiar English activity – the preservation society. As you can imagine, activists met dogged opposition from government and local authorities but they refused to go away and, today, we must thank them for our restored canal system, our working mills and engines and, of course, our working preserved railways. We live in a rich society, which has both time and money to indulge in interests apart from work. The reawakened interest in these earlier feats of engineering is for everybody. Unless you are already a railway fan, you may be surprised to learn that in England alone we have some 120 railway preservation sites.

FIG 2.13: *New track being laid, not by Network Rail, but by volunteers on the reclaimed track bed of a long-closed rural line. Ahead the track bed has been cleared and ballasted and the concrete sleepers laid, awaiting the next section of rail. (GWR)*

29

These vary from small collections, to steam railway lines that run a full timetable of trains over many miles of track. It has been very popular in TV dramas to include a shot involving steam trains and these are not film sets but simply our restored lines, albeit with carefully changed station names. It is these sites that provide the bulk of the photographs for this book and allow us to see how things were done in the years when steam reigned supreme.

FIG 2.14: *A coach, somewhat the worse for wear, awaiting restoration. Most pre-1950 coaching stock was built in wood on steel frames and restoration demands considerable skill. (DRC)*

FIG 2.15: *Step back in time – Hampton Loade station on the Severn Valley Railway. Just how important these rural stations were can be gauged from the fact that the local village population was less than 500 but look how grand the station is! Note the sleepers across the tracks – very few country stations were built with bridges or subways to link the platforms. (SVR)*

SECTION II

WHERE
SHALL
WE GO?

CHAPTER 3

Surveying and Planning the Route

W e have mentioned the perils of surveying the very earliest lines and the problems of getting an Act through Parliament, but what of the engineers' work? Just how did they plan a railway line?

The process was usually started by local tradespeople wanting to improve their profits by achieving lower costs. Transport, both of the materials coming into and the goods leaving an area, is often a significant portion of these costs. A secondary driving force, particularly for the later railways, was 'keeping up with the Joneses'. This tended to involve local landowners and dignitaries who wanted their area to be seen as successful and modern.

Having banded together and decided that a railway was what they needed, the promoters had to raise interest and money. Subscriptions were invited and the next step was to get a surveyor to see if a route between the chosen areas was practical and what its likely costs would be. In the case of most lines, there wasn't much in the way of maps or, more importantly, geophysical data for the surveyor to work on. The other dramatically limiting factor was that the early locomotive could not haul a useful load up any gradient steeper than around 1 in 150. George Stephenson suggested 1 in 200 as the

ideal limit. Though the engines improved rapidly, many of the key main lines were surveyed with these modest gradients in mind. Brunel, for instance, when planning the Great Western line from London to Bristol, achieved half the route at 1 in 1,000 and most of the rest at better than 1 in 750, though a short section used a 1 in 100 gradient.

Let's consider Fig 3.1. The task is to link town A to town B, and the promoters have asked for the fastest and the cheapest route – we can all dream!

The fastest route will involve a mix of low gradients and as short a distance as possible – exactly the mix Brunel set himself in the London to Bristol route. The first job is to determine the height difference and the distance between A and B; we can then see what the gradient would be if we followed a completely straight route, Route 1. For the sake of the discussion, let's say the distance apart is 10 miles and the difference in height is 50 ft. The straight line (Route 1) gradient would therefore be 50 in 10 x 5,280 (feet in a mile) or 1 in 1,000, which is virtually flat. The problem is the earthworks needed – two tunnels, an embankment nearly a mile long and four cuttings. A very expensive option.

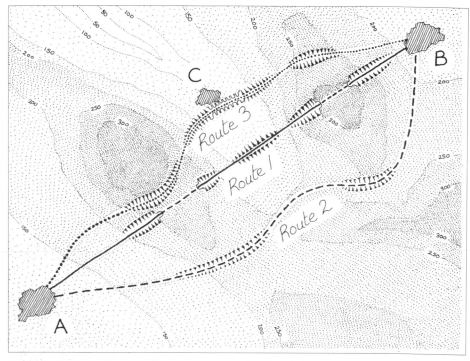

FIG 3.1: *Map to illustrate the route choices that faced the surveyor.*

Now look at Route 2, the dashed line that represents the best compromise. This climbs to the 200 ft level (taking 2 miles at 1 in 210) and then stays more or less level until town B. The new line has not needed any substantial embankments or tunnels and just two cuttings. The gradients are still well within the most conservative recom- mendations; the only penalty is that the distance is now around 13 miles. One could juggle with the route, taking a straighter line and possibly using a short tunnel to reduce the overall distance. In practice the surveyor would have clashed with landowners, who would have forced some other alterations, plus the residents of town C would have been jumping up and down to have the line pass through their town as well. The dotted line (Route 3) would achieve this, though it would mean gradients around the 1 in 180 mark, cuttings and embankments and one fairly short tunnel. The question for both the surveyor and the company is – would town C produce sufficient traffic to cover these extra costs?

The point of this exercise is to try and show how the surveyor could balance the length of the route, the gradients and the expensive earthworks. It also shows why so many of the 'cheap to build' rural lines wandered around, avoiding hills and valleys while still trying to reach every village on the way.

The other point we must remember is that virtually all lines were surveyed and built at a time of great competition. The first on the scene took the best position and those who followed had to make do.

In very hilly areas there was one other weapon the surveyor could use to keep the costs low and that was to use a narrow track gauge. This enabled much tighter turns to be used, which meant the line could follow contours without heavy cuttings or embankments. Many mineral lines and quite a few passenger-carrying lines were built in smaller gauges. One metre, 3 ft, 2 ft, plus several other odd sizes, were employed, particularly on the Continent and in America. In England, many quarry lines used narrow gauges but only two were constructed as proper passenger and goods lines – the

FIG 3.2: *It's not often that you can see an obvious gradient on a railway but here on the Looe branch in Cornwall it's all too obvious! The single coach diesel unit has arrived from Looe and after pulling forward over the point and reversing, it will set off up the 1 in 40 climb to Liskeard station.*

much loved but sadly long-gone line from Barnstable to Lynton in Devon using the 2 ft gauge, and the equally missed Leek and Manifold in Staffordshire.

Incidentally I have used the nominal gauges in this book; the actual gauge was often slightly different. Brunel's 7 ft was in practice 7 ft ¼ inch, while the Lynton line, like many of the Welsh narrow gauge lines, was 1 ft 11½ inches.

FIG 3.3: *The type of terrain that makes narrow gauge lines useful. A British-built Beyer Garratt articulated locomotive gently eases its train around the western slopes of Snowdon. These ex-South African Railways machines are the largest 2 ft gauge locomotives in the world. (WHR)*

FIG 3.4: *So difficult was the route for the Great Western as it battled up the River Dee gorge that even the station, here in Llangollen, had barely a yard of platform that wasn't on a curve.*

FIG 3.5: *Gradient boards are used to indicate a change in the gradient of the track. The letter L simply means level and the number means 1 ft rise in every 99 ft of distance. (WSR)*

FIG 3.6: *Another Cornish branch line built with severe gradients – restored Great Western class 4200, built in 1916, draws its train up the 1 in 40 climb towards Bodmin General station in Cornwall. (BWR)*

Keeping A Level

The building of cuttings, embankments, bridges and tunnels had been well practised on the canals, built 50 or more years before the railways. Nevertheless, the main line railways were often built on a grander scale and such structures were bigger and longer than their canal relatives, demanding great daring and skill.

Early embankments and cuttings had the habit of slipping, as if nature was trying to get back to where it started. Greater knowledge of soil mechanics largely solved this problem but, if the ground was poor, or full of wet clay, sand or loose shale, then brick or stone supporting walls were built to hold the soil at bay. We must also remember that

FIG 4.1: *The cutting near the top of the Lickey incline, south of Birmingham. The sides have been reinforced to retain the loose soil, probably when the original two tracks were widened to four.*

all this work was still done by men with wheelbarrows, though the technique of using the soil removed from a cutting to create the next embankment was well understood. The author well remembers the first motorways being built and the announcement on TV that they had worked out this brilliant new idea of using the spoil from the cuttings to build the embankments, just as the railways and canals had done over 150 years before!

Tunnels were the biggest problem. Test bores down into the line of a tunnel were not easy to do in the early 19th century and sometimes the

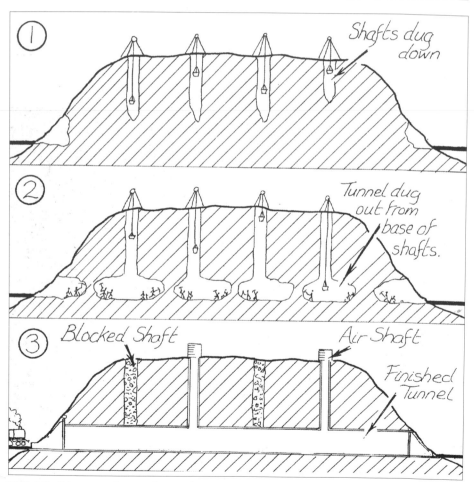

FIG 4.2: *Diagram of typical tunnel construction showing how shafts were sunk to provide several working faces.*

engineer would find quicksand or excessive water once they had started into a hill. I'll give two examples to illustrate the problem.

On the LNWR London to Birmingham line a 1½-mile-long tunnel was needed at Kilsby. In the parliamentary stages, Robert Stephenson said of the tunnel: 'Very easy indeed, in all clays it is very easy to tunnel, unless they be a great deal mixed with sand.' In practice he hit quicksand and it took 18 months to construct just 600 yards, using pumps night and day to remove the water. When the Great Western obtained its Act in 1872 to build a 4½ mile tunnel under the River Severn, little did the engineers know what awaited them. They had assumed that the most difficult section would be under the deepest part of the Severn, where the tunnel was to be 45 ft below the riverbed but, in practice, their greatest problem was a spring that burst into the tunnel in 1879, completely flooding the workings. It took nearly a year to pump the working dry enough for men to restart work

FIG 4.3: *The northern portal of the notorious Kilsby Tunnel, viewed through the maze of overhead electric wires. The tunnel is having work done on it and the train services are suspended on this bright June morning. Note how large the tunnel is, the tall elliptical shape not only imparts strength but allows room for the engine smoke to disperse.*

and, in 1881, the two headings, working out from either bank, met. Two years later, while work was still in progress on the tunnel, the 'great spring' broke through again. This time one of the largest pumps also failed plus a large tidal wave breached the surface workings, trapping 83 men, who were later rescued by boat. A new side heading was cut, into which the spring was diverted and pumps have removed the water ever since. What was, at the time, the world's longest underwater tunnel finally opened in 1886 – it had taken 13 years to complete.

By far the most exciting structures are the bridges, very visible and sometimes slightly frightening. Many techniques have been used but brick or stone arches are the most common in England, with concrete being cautiously tried late in the 19th century. Wood, iron and, later, steel provide some of the most spectacular bridges and viaducts, though only three wooden examples are left, two in Wales and one in Scotland.

Finding good solid ground to support the arches was always the problem and this usually meant digging down until rock was met; sheer hard work on land, but a problem when taking a bridge across water. Brunel faced this when taking the Great Western Railway from

FIG 4.4: *A classic stone viaduct, this is the Moorswater viaduct in Cornwall. Over 300 yds long and standing some 147 ft high, it was built in 1881. The free-standing pillars are the remains of the original 1857 wooden viaduct.*

FIG 4.5: *Possibly the most iconic bridge in England, Brunel's crossing of the River Tamar between Devon and Cornwall. Built to carry just one track, it now forms the only railway link between England and Cornwall. The great height above the river was a requirement of the Admiralty, to permit high-masted boats to pass underneath. The centre tower stands in about 80 ft of water.*

Devon into Cornwall across the River Tamar, just west of Plymouth. The Admiralty demanded that the bridge should give clearance to tall-masted ships; so Brunel had quite a challenge. He made use of wrought iron to construct the bridge, using an unusual design of two great bow sections from which the track was suspended. Brunel had always distrusted cast iron, though it was used by many others prior to the mid 1800s. Wrought iron eventually gave way to steel in bridge construction by the end of the 19th century, usually riveted and, after the 1950s, welded. Lift or swing bridges were often demanded to allow river or dock traffic to pass in situations where it would have been almost impossible, or very expensive, to raise the railway high enough to use a fixed bridge (see Fig 4.8).

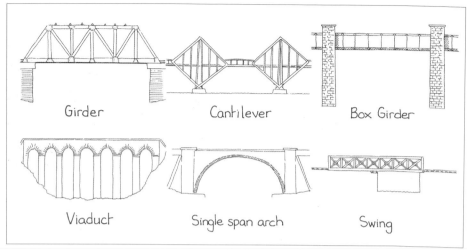

Girder   Cantilever   Box Girder

Viaduct   Single span arch   Swing

FIG 4.6: *Diagram of the basic bridge types used in railway construction.*

FIG 4.7: *In 1874 the London and South Western Railway completed its route between Exeter and Plymouth by going round the north side of Dartmoor. This is the 120 ft high Meldon viaduct, one of just two to use wrought iron truss construction in England and now a Scheduled Ancient Monument. Just to the right is Meldon Quarry and the end of the Dartmoor Railway.*

FIG 4.8: *Three for the price of one! The longest wooden bridge in Britain, taking the old Cambrian Railways line across the Mawddach estuary, near Barmouth. At this end is an iron bowstring girder swing bridge, which was operational up to 1987 and allowed masted boats to sail further inland. Gently moving over the bridge is a steam train, part of a regular steam-hauled service run along this line in the summer.*

FIG 4.9: *Virtually all the steam trains running on the Severn Valley line cross the Victoria Bridge over the River Severn, making it probably the busiest large iron span bridge used by steam trains in the country. (SVR)*

CHAPTER 5

The Roadway

The ground that carried the tracks had to fulfil only two criteria – to stay in place and bear the weight. Like all innocent statements, this belies the problems that Nature throws at the civil engineer. In practice, though, a fairly standard arrangement has evolved whereby stone ballast absorbs the impact of passing trains and aids the removal of heavy rain. Drain ditches, usually stone-filled, are the other key ingredients. In cuttings, these drainage channels are often taken up the sides of the cutting and also along the tops to remove surface water before it gets the chance to run down into the cutting.

The rail itself changed remarkably little, simply growing in strength and size. The advent of mass steel production brought a vast increase in the life of the rail; wrought iron track lasted only a matter of months on busy lines, whereas the new steel rails lasted over ten years. The use of sleepers, again, changed very little. The materials varied, as did the means of holding the rail in place, but, while Robert Stephenson might be amazed at some of the changes, he would certainly recognise modern track as a natural development of that used in the 1830s.

Originally some thought the track should be as rigid as possible and Brunel took this approach at one stage, but experience showed that it needed to be able to flex a little. If you stand near to modern track when a heavy locomotive goes by, you will probably be alarmed to see just how much the track dips beneath the wheels. This is part of the reason track ballast is kept loose and clean – glance at any of the remaining unused sidings or lines where the soil has compacted and become weed-filled to see the

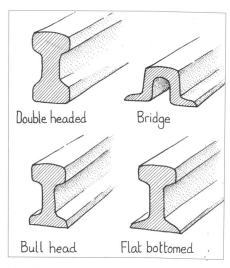

FIG 5.1: *Drawing showing four of the rail sections used. The double-headed rail was intended to be reversible once one surface had worn down. The bridge rail was used in the early GWR days. Today, all new track is flat bottomed though bull-head rail is still standard on most preserved lines.*

FIG 5.2: *The top-hat section bridge rail used for Brunel's original broad gauge lines. (DRC)*

difference. Railtrack renew something like three million tons of ballast each year to keep the track properly supported.

Today, most preserved lines still have bull-head track but since the 1940s our main lines have followed Europe and America in using flat-bottomed rail held to the sleepers by clips. For many years, rail was produced in 60 ft lengths and joined by two plates (fishplates) bolted through the two rail ends, this joint giving rise to the classic 'de-dum-de-dum' noise of wheels crossing the gaps. This joint also allowed for the expansion and contraction of the rail as the weather changed. Dramatic evidence of this effect came from Canada, where a line was exposed to enormous heat in a forest fire, and the track lifted from the ballast and ended up twisted like some giant snake. Early in the 20th century, it was realised that, at least here in Britain, if the track was

FIG 5.3: *Siding track which hasn't been maintained but which is still regularly used at very low speeds.*

FIG 5.4: *Joint in bull-head rail showing the twin wires which give electrical continuity across the joint.*

FIG 5.5: *A steel spring and a wooden wedge holding bull-head rail into the chairs. Because the springs or wedges can fall out the track is regularly inspected. (DRC)*

pre-tensioned and held in more closely spaced sleepers, the expansion could be contained. This allowed the rail lengths to be welded into long sections, though a sliding joint is still used to take up some movement.

Bull-head rail is held in a cast chair which, in turn, is screwed to the wooden sleepers. A wooden wedge or, more recently, a steel spring holds the rail tight in the chair. Today, the sleepers are normally concrete with 'Pandrol' clips holding the rail.

Before leaving the basic track work we must look at the problems of going round corners. On main lines, where higher speeds are involved, it is normal to tilt the track on curves to compensate for the outward centrifugal

FIG 5.6: *Flat-bottomed rail held by Pandrol clips. The vast majority of the UK's railways use this type of rail. (LL)*

force. This prevents the wheel flanges from rubbing against the rails – it also stops your coffee cup from sliding across the table as you glide along at 100 mph. When travelling in a train that is going around such curves at a slow speed, you become aware that the train is tilting, a most strange feeling.

We must now look at the basic mechanism that lies behind the use of an edge rail. It's easy to assume that the wheel flanges keep the train in place but this is not so. The running surface of the wheel is not flat to the ground but slopes, so that the point at which it rests on the top of the rail determines the working diameter of the wheel and, in turn, the active circumference. The wheels are fixed to their axle, so if the left-hand wheel moves left of its rail, the right-hand wheel will be moving to the left of its rail. This movement means that the left-hand wheel is now running at a point of greater diameter (A) whilst the right-hand wheel is running at a smaller diameter (B). The left-hand wheel therefore covers a greater distance per revolution than the right-hand wheel. In effect, it tries to overtake the right-hand wheel, which

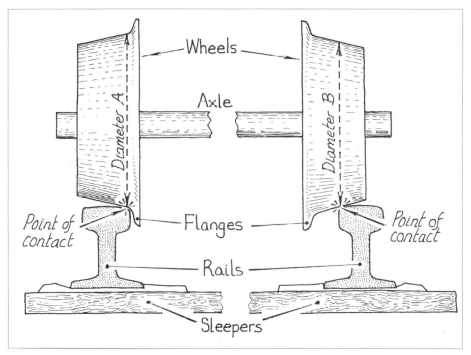

FIG 5.7: *A somewhat exaggerated drawing to show how their sloping profile automatically centres the wheels. In practice, the slope is far less and the wheel sits roughly on the centre of the rail top.*

FIG 5.8: *Basic points, shown set for the right-hand track. Near to the camera is the 'frog', where the flange on the wheels is able to pass through a gap in the rail. Opposite this crossing, on each side, are the check rails that prevent a wheel taking the wrong track. As this is only a siding, the points are hand-operated by the lever next to the blade end.*

causes the axle to turn slightly back towards the point where both wheels are running on the same diameter. This movement will always try to centre the wheels on the track; the flanges don't come into action at all. Now, when the train goes round a curve, one side must cover a greater distance – the outside of a curve must be a greater distance than the inside, otherwise it wouldn't be a curve. The wheels simply move over, so that they work on different diameters, allowing the wheel on the outside of the curve to travel further in distance. There is obviously a finite

limit to this effect. The tighter the curve, the further over the wheel has to move, and eventually it will reach the flange, which will rub along the rail, producing the awful screech that we sometimes hear when a train goes round a very tight curve. The flange is now serving its real purpose, that of safety, keeping the wheels on the track when other forces would try to derail it.

This neatly brings us to the other fundamental rail formation: the point, needed to allow a train to have a choice of tracks to follow. Immediately we have a problem – how to let the wheel

FIG 5.9: *A double slip point where any track can be set to any other track. These are used primarily in sidings and other slow speed areas, where they save space. (DRC)*

FIG 5.10: *The simplest form of interlocking. The wire which operates the adjacent signal passes through the interlock frame (marked X), which will block its movement unless the point blade is fully set correctly. (DRC)*

flanges cross over a rail. The answer is to make a gap which the wheel simply has to bump across. As the wheel does this, there is a moment when it could, in theory at least, turn the wrong way and to prevent this we make use of the flange. This time, though, it's the of the other wheel that is retained short length of rail called a check which prevents the axle from leaving the chosen route. The choice of which way the train will turn is made by the tapered point blades which are set hard over either to the right or to the left, and it is these blades that move when the point is set. We now have to address a safety issue. It would be catastrophic if the point blades were to move when a train was crossing over or, heaven forbid, for the blades not to move in unison. To prevent these situations, the two blades are joined securely and a mechanism used which 'proves' that both have moved before the signals can be set. In fact, this idea of interlocking the point work to the signals is fundamental to the safety of our railways.

Point work soon grew to include crossings and more complex-looking layouts. Slips are a clever space-saving point, where a cross-over and two or four points are combined. Three-way points, which are, in fact, only two

FIG 5.11: *Classic branch line station. This is Williton, where 1928-built* Small Prairie *5553 simmers with its train. (WSR)*

separate points built very close together, were another popular space-saving arrangement.

The last of the static features we need before we can think of running our trains are the buildings – the stations, goods yards and engine sheds.

Stations have not changed their function over the years; they are basically a place where people can join or leave a train. In England, we usually have a raised platform that runs the length of the train so no matter where the train stops people can easily reach a coach door, and those leaving aren't faced with a 3 ft drop. The next feature is some form of shelter to protect passengers waiting for a train. This varies from something not much more th n an open-front shed to a warm n with seating. Visit some of the lines in the winter and you will a real coal fire burning as well! F. n the early days of long-distance travel, two other features became vital: toilets and hot drinks. Trains didn't have corridors or toilets until the late 19th century so from the start these features were essential. Intermediate stops were also used to refresh

FIG 5.12: *Pride and style! Stone station on the old North Staffordshire Railway, is a Grade II listed building. Designed by Sir Henry Hunt and opened in 1849, it is now passed on both sides by high speed trains.*

heaters – well, earthenware flasks filled with hot water, as there was no heating on early trains either. Once trains had toilets, food and heating, they could undertake much longer journeys without stopping, but the traveller still expected to find these facilities at all stations, regardless of size. Stations were also the point at which tickets were issued and could be checked, along with providing the space needed to handle passengers' luggage. Most of the working restored steam lines have stations that appear to be frozen in time, and are absolutely beautiful.

Specific traffic such as stone, coal, etc, was often the reason a line was built, but very quickly the type of goods people wanted to move expanded to cover all manner of things. Goods services developed an amazing range of special wagons, along with the facilities

Right: the long forgotten platform ticket machine. Far right bottom: No computer screens here, just simple changeable destination boards.

FIG 5.13: *Preserved stations are awash with useful bits and pieces, many of which will seem strange to modern eyes. This figure, plus Figs 5.14 and 5.15, shows a typical selection. (SVR)*

FIG 5.14: *A much rarer feature – a coffin carrier in tasteful black, used to move coffins between hearse and train. (BR)*

The GWR never missed a trick – their initials are worked into these seat bases. (GWR)

And below a portable weighing machine. Carriage was often charged for by weight.

Water carriers to refresh toilet flushing water on the coaches.

FIG 5.15: *A further selection of typical country station features, including the friendly booking office at Rolvenden. Massive station names like this example from Sheffield Park, were taken down during the war and rarely survived. And just imagine London to Brighton return for 12 shillings (60p)! (KESR, WSR, BR)*

to handle them. Virtually every station had a bay platform or a goods shed where general packages could be loaded or unloaded, plus a cattle dock where livestock could be handled and a coal yard. It's hard to imagine just how big some of these depots were. In Birmingham, the GWR had a massive goods facility just north of Snow Hill station, nearly half a mile long, from which horse-drawn wagons flowed almost continuously. The LMS and the LNER had similar facilities near the city centre as well. These yards handled mostly general goods; in addition factories, dairies and coal merchants all

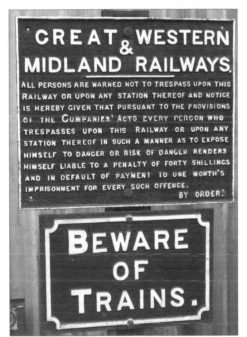

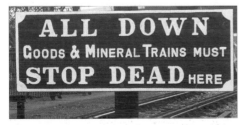

FIG 5.16: *Signs are another common feature. Somehow the old cast iron signs seem so much more interesting than modern ones. (DFR, DRC, SVR)*

FIG 5.17: *Loading bays, where goods could be loaded directly into a wagon. Along with a coal yard these were found at every station of any size. (SDR)*

FIG 5.18: *Cattle docks, where livestock could be organised and loaded into special cattle wagons. These were common in rural areas. (BRC)*

had their own sidings. Nearly all these have now completely disappeared, as the lorry handles these goods more easily and cheaply than rail. Again, the restored railways give us a glimpse of this activity with its colourful private owners' wagons, and occasionally they run complete demonstration goods trains.

FIG 5.19: *Short siding serving a loading bay complete with a crane which would have lifted goods between horse-drawn carts and the goods trucks. (SVR)*

FIG 5.20: *Museum display of a typical horse-drawn cart that would have carried all manner of goods to and from station loading bays. (BRC)*

CHAPTER 6

Who Goes First?

The very early railways operated by a system of timing, trains leaving a station at least ten minutes after the previous service. Lineside policemen would have clocks so that they could slow down or stop a train if it arrived at their position before the ten minutes had elapsed. These men also had to check the track and keep people off the line and they weren't always as vigilant as they might have been.

FIG 6.1: *Very early rotating signal shown in its 'safe to pass' position. A pulley and chain system enables the signal to be raised or lowered. (DRC)*

It doesn't take much imagination to see problems with this simple scheme: if a train broke down out of sight of a policeman, he would wave on the next train oblivious to the danger. Very quickly this system was improved by having signal posts that carried a wide variety of arms, discs or even oil lamps. These would be set, still by a man on the ground, to warn of danger ahead. It was assumed that if there was no danger indicated, then it was safe to proceed; that is, the absence of a warning signal was taken as 'safe'. This meant that if the signal was faulty, or, as in one accident, frozen, it couldn't indicate danger – there was no fail-safe mechanism, there was no need to prove it was safe.

The dangers were soon realised and, by the mid 19th century the semaphore signal became standard. This has just two states – stop or pass. The clever bit is that if the wire operating the signal arm breaks, the arm always returns to the stop position. These arms were also mounted on a bearing that couldn't be jammed by snow or ice. Most lines adopted the arm being raised to indicate 'safe to pass' but the GWR chose the reverse – the arm dropped for safe. The weight of the arm, however, was such that it would still move to the horizontal 'stop' position should the operating wire break.

There is a potential problem in using

FIG 6.2: *Working 'slot' signal. Because the signal arm drops into the slot for the 'safe to pass' position, it can become frozen in its slot, giving a continuous clear indication regardless of any danger. (DRC)*

friction, a separate weight is fitted close to the signal arm which ensures that any wire friction is overcome. This makes it harder to pull the signal lever and, to prevent the weights bouncing, the signalman has to develop a technique involving a small pause halfway through the lever movement.

Points are operated by rods that can provide a 'push-pull' motion, involving considerably more force than operating a signal.

We still had the problem of how to know the previous train was not in the way and this was solved by the idea of the block system. Here, as now, the line

a wire to pull a signal into the 'safe to pass' position. Suppose the wire has to travel a considerable distance to the signal. Its path is formed by a series of pulleys plus several cranks, all of which can become dry and reluctant to let the wire move freely. So when the signalman releases the lever to set the signal back to danger, the signal arm has to drag the wire back along the pulleys, a far too dangerous task. To ensure the wire isn't held by the pulley

FIG 6.3: *Classic lower quadrant signal, which drops to indicate that it's safe to pass. Note the access ladders, the safety rail and the balance weight. The white diamond means this section of track also has electrical track circuits to detect the presence of a train. (SVR)*

FIG 6.4: *A very rare somersault signal. The arm pivots in the centre and the spectacle carrying the red and green filters for the light has its own pivot near the top of the post. (NVR)*

FIG 6.5: *Modern electric signals.*

is split up into sections, called blocks, and the traffic is checked when it enters and when it leaves a section. Only one train is allowed in a section at any one time – but how do you let the signalman at the start of a block know that the previous train has left the section and that it is now empty and able to accept another train? Enter the telegraph. Early work with electricity had reached the point where it was possible to send simple on/off signals over long distances and this was used to link the signalmen along a line. By now the signalmen had a signal box, where all the points and signals could be operated by one man, who controlled and coordinated his area. This naturally tended to be at a station, since

FIG 6.6: *Inside a typical signal box. The levers operate the points and signals, often being colour-coded to show their function. Each lever has a label that gives its purpose. The short trigger in front of each lever handle releases a locking mechanism that ensures the lever is locked in position and not left halfway. The row of boxes and polished brass knobs are the signal repeaters and the telegraph signals to show which sections of track are clear and to communicate with the next signal box. (SVR)*

this was where sidings and junctions were usually built. He could still get it wrong, however. The system relied on the signalman remembering where the trains were and not setting the signals to a route not selected by the points. This last safety issue was also solved at the same time by mechanically inter-locking the levers so that a conflicting route could not be set. We now had the signalling system that was to serve virtually right up to the present day.

One special extra was introduced, mainly for single-track lines, where a token was carried by the engine driver which acted as his permission to be on a specific block or section of the line. These tokens fit into machines in the signal boxes, which are linked by an electrical circuit which prevents more than one token being issued for a section at any one time. If you visit almost any of the busy restored steam lines, you will see the driver and signalman exchange tokens as a train arrives at a station.

Signal boxes grew to enormous size at the large junctions, as did the

FIG 6.7: *Token machines in the Bridgenorth signal box. To exchange the token with the train driver, the token is clipped into a large loop, which makes it easy to collect from the signalman. Incidentally, many 'signalmen' are women. (SVR)*

FIG 6.8: *Below the signal box is the interlocking room, where a wonderful machine hides. Each lever passes through the frame, and cross bars ensure that a wrong or dangerous route cannot be set or signalled. (GCR)*

FIG 6.9: *The signalman prepares to exchange tokens with the incoming train. He is holding the new token in his right hand for the crew to take and he will collect the old token from the fireman with his left hand as the engine goes past. (WSR)*

FIG 6.10: *Point-operating rods and signal operating wires emerge from the signal box. Cranks are used to change the direction of the rods and pulleys for the signal wires. (KESR)*

FIG 6.11: *Level crossing gates that are still opened and closed from the signal box, once standard practice but now relatively unusual. (NVR)*

FIG 6.12: *Inside the signal box, showing the wheel used to operate the gates. The four levers control the locking mechanisms on the gates, needed to prevent accidental movement while a train is near and to interlock the signals. (NVR)*

complexity of the signal gantries carrying the semaphore signals.

As I mentioned in the history section, non-mechanical signalling had appeared by the start of the 20th century and electric light signals soon became adopted as standard, being slowly introduced as refurbishment was carried out. Track circuits are used to detect when a train is on a section; so signalmen no longer need to visually check the passing of a train. These detect the short circuit between the rails caused by the wheels simply being on the track; this means that any wagon or coach on a line will show up and indicate that the section is occupied. Point work also became electrically operated, so now our signal box no longer needed any mechanical levers, as everything was done by switches and all the interlocking functions were controlled by relays. In fact, the signal box of old is no longer needed at all. Today we have faceless machine rooms, and signalmen only intervene when there is something out of the ordinary to control.

FIG 6.13: *Restored signal box, complete with stove and adjacent storage huts. The windows allow the signalman to see all his signals and the trains. (BWR)*

FIG 6.14: *Some people keep gnomes in their gardens but here we have a selection of ground signals. These would have been used to signal local or shunting movements, usually within the limits of a station. (CPRR)*

FIG 6.15: *Though the enormous signal gantries of the 1900s have all gone, many preserved lines still have impressive arrays of semaphore signals in their stations. (ELR)*

Section III

The
Wonderful
Wheel

CHAPTER 7

The Mighty Locomotive

This leaves us with the glamorous part of the railways, the locomotives. First, let's run through the basics of the steam engine. If water is heated in a sealed container, once the water reaches its boiling point, steam is given off, which, occupying some 1,600 times the space of the water it came from, causes a pressure to be built up. This increased pressure, in fact, stops the water boiling or, rather, it increases the temperature at which the water will boil and produce more steam. Thus, for any given source of heat, there will be a natural pressure that the steam will reach. If we remove some of the steam to do work, then the pressure will drop and the water will start to boil again until the natural balance is regained.

The cylinders are where this pressure is turned into motion in any reciprocating steam engine and our locomotives are no exception. The cylinder is fitted with a piston, which makes a good seal to the cylinder walls

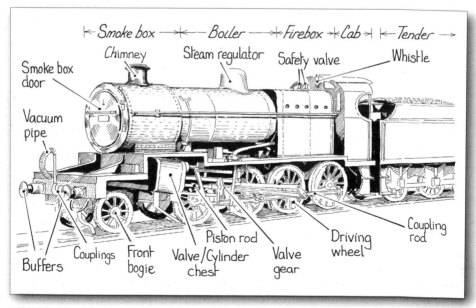

FIG 7.1: *This drawing based on a Somerset and Dorset Joint Railway locomotive, built in 1925, identifies the main parts. (WSR)*

FIG 7.2: *The awe-inspiring sight of 100 tons of steam-driven machinery getting under way captures the magic of the steam locomotive. This is 9F* Black Prince, *owned by artist David Shepherd. (GWR)*

but is free to move to and fro. Fitted to the piston is a rod, which passes out of one end of the cylinder – this is where the work of moving the engine starts. First though, we have to make the piston move to and fro within the cylinder, using the steam pressure from the boiler. Steam is let into the cylinder behind the piston; this pushes the piston down the cylinder. Just before it reaches the end, the valve that admitted the steam is closed. During this power phase, another valve is opened to let the air or steam escape from in front of the advancing piston, usually up the chimney. Now the same process is used

but the steam enters at the other end, where the piston has just come to rest, and pushes it back again to be released at the end of that stroke. This sequence is simply repeated over and over again. Having got our rod going to and fro, we connect it to one of the wheels by a crank that works rather like our leg when pedalling a bicycle, causing the wheel to turn.

Oh, if life was that simple!

Turning that perfectly true account of a steam engine into a working machine involves solving many problems. I won't dwell on the remarkable learning curve that the likes of Robert

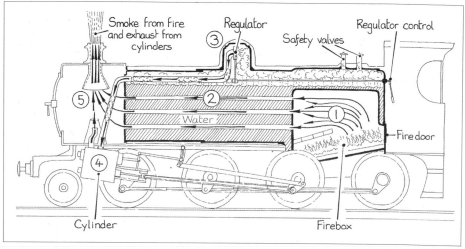

FIG 7.3: *Cross-section of an earlier locomotive showing the basic parts.*

1. *Hot air and smoke from the fire drawn into the smoke tubes.*
2. *This heats the water, producing steam which collects above the water level.*
3. *The steam escapes through the regulator valve, down into the cylinders.*
4. *The steam is used to push the piston to and fro before leaving.*
5. *Exhaust steam from the cylinders shoots up the chimney, drawing the smoke from the fire with it.*

Stephenson climbed back in the 1830s, but instead will describe in greater detail the various parts of the locomotives that we can still see working today.

First, the frames – rarely seen but vital. These are formed from two steel plates, usually around an inch thick which, with cross members, form what in car terms would be the chassis. The main driving wheel axles are carried on bearings, which, in turn, sit in guides mounted to the frames. Any front or rear bogies are also fitted to the frames. The boiler, firebox and cab are mounted on top of the frames, and all the valve gear and the cylinders are also mounted onto the frames.

The boiler and its companion, the firebox, form the largest components and indeed are the most obvious parts to the eye. Two features had been realised quite early on. Firstly, if the fumes and smoke from the fire are taken through the boiler in many small tubes, this transfers the maximum heat from the fire to the water. Secondly, if the firebox is surrounded by water, this heats the water up as well. In fact, more heating takes place from this than from the boiler tubes. The fire is actually a relatively complex feature. It must

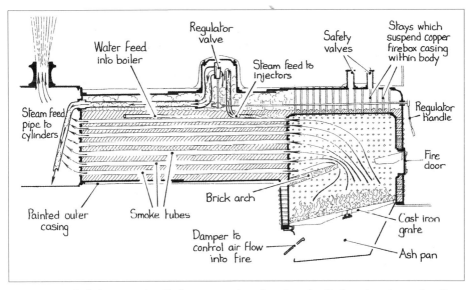

FIG 7.4: *A slightly more detailed cross-section showing the firebox in greater detail. Earlier locomotives had straight boilers and the characteristic high dome over the regulator valve.*

achieve the heat needed but at a continuous rate – you can't wait for steam while fresh coal that has been put on the fire catches light and builds up heat. Nor can you wait while the ashes and clinker are cleaned out and the fire relit. The fire must burn for several hours, ideally all day, and its heat output must be controllable. An engine tackling a ten-mile climb will need much more steam than when simply coasting down the same ten miles. Lastly, we want to extract every last possible bit of heat from the coal. By the end of the 19th century, the best solution had been evolved and the same basic design lasted to the end of steam.

At this point, I must start using diagrams to explain what is going on, in particular, cross-section drawings. If you are unfamiliar with this technique, imagine an orange cut in half. Now hold one half with the cut surface facing you, and what you see is a cross section taken through the centre of the fruit. Whilst a touch obvious, note that you can now see so much more – pips, the sectional construction, the pith, all features that were completely hidden when looking at the whole. Cross-section drawings are commonly taken through the centre of the object and that is true of those in this book.

Fig 7.4 shows a drawing of the firebox, boiler and chimney of a typical locomotive. The fire burns on a long, wide grate (usually of cast iron bars), which slopes slightly downwards to

FIG 7.5: *Two boilers, complete with their fireboxes, awaiting major overhaul work. These are both early locomotives with straight boilers and tall regulator assemblies. Note the hundreds of firebox stays and the diminutive fire door, through which the fireman feeds coal onto the fire. (BR)*

make the task of getting the coal to the far end easier. On modern locomotives the grate itself can be agitated by a lever in the cab, which allows the fireman to clear the ash and most of the clinker down into the ash pan below. The fire is normally about 6 to 8 inches deep (15–20 cm), the coal being 'thrown', using a shovel, through an opening covered by the fire door. Some locomotives have a pair of doors, some are opened by a pedal and a steam piston.

Above the fire itself is a brick arch, which forms a roof over the fire and forces the smoke and fumes to flow towards the cab before turning round and moving towards the smoke tubes in the boiler. This arch and the path the smoke takes are very important – a second flow of air is admitted above the fire door, which mixes with the hot fumes, causing a second burning phase. This time, though, it is the carbon and sulphur which burns, leaving the fumes much cleaner and, of course, hotter still. In fact, more heat is produced in this second burning phase than comes directly from the burning coal.

FIG 7.6: *Inside the smoke box of a 1937-built, LMS 'Black Five' locomotive. The blast pipe is at the bottom of the picture, with the petticoat that forms the start of the chimney above. Behind this is the end of the boiler showing the smoke tubes, through which the smoke from the fire is drawn. The smaller pipes rising up are the superheating tubes and the two large pipes are the two main steam pipes, which pass down to the valves and cylinders. The small pipe feeding into the blast pipe (bottom) is the steam blower. This smokebox has had all the self-cleaning plates removed for work, giving this unusual view. (GCR)*

These hot fumes now pass through the boiler tubes to emerge in the smoke box at the front of the engine. Here the odd unburnt particles, plus general ash and soot, fall to the bottom whilst the rest of the fumes rise up the chimney. This debris can become moist and very corrosive. Some smoke boxes have a brick or concrete layer at the bottom to prevent the ash mix from touching the steelwork. Others have a wire mesh screen, which, along with other plates, causes turbulence that breaks up any clinker and allows the resultant ash to be forced through the chimney. These are classed as self-cleaning smoke boxes and carry a 'SC' sign on the smoke box door. The smoke box has an airtight door, which can be opened to clear out the smoke box; also the smoke tubes that run through the boiler can be accessed for cleaning, using extremely long flue brushes. The GWR used a steam lance (a long tube down which steam was driven) for this job.

Now, as anyone who has struggled to get a coal fire burning will know, the fumes and gases don't follow this convoluted journey willingly. Nor does coal burn bright and hot unless it has plenty of air passing through it. When moving, air is pushed through a damper door below the fire grate to feed the fire directly, but getting it through the boiler tubes still requires help, so the exhaust steam from the cylinders is sent up the chimney via a blast pipe and this provides the main draw for the fire.

When lighting the fire from cold at the start of a working day, great care is needed not to get the fire going too quickly – time must be allowed for the firebox and the boiler to heat up and expand evenly. In fact, the boiler is bolted to the locomotive frames only at the front; the firebox end has provision to slide to and fro as the boiler expands due to heating. On a typical main line locomotive this expansion can move the firebox, along with all the controls, around 5/8th of an inch (15mm). Most locomotives have a pipe in the shape of a ring (blower ring) that allows steam to be directed up the chimney to maintain a draw when the engine is stationary. The cleaning of both the fire grate and the smoke box at the end of a working day, plus the hours it takes next morning to get the fire alight and steam up to pressure, are among the major disadvantages of steam com-

pared to diesel or electric locomotives.

In order to surround the fire with water, the firebox is made of two boxes spaced around 4 inches (10cm) apart. The outside is steel but the inside is made of a hard grade of copper (arsenical copper) and this is held in place by hundreds of stays – short steel bolts which pass between the outer steel case and the copper firebox. All of this has not just to be watertight but to be watertight under the pressure of the steam, no easy task.

The water itself fills the boiler nearly to the top, and extends over the top of the firebox. This is rather important since the copper firebox would soften and fail should the top be uncovered. The water has to be pumped from the tender (most of the tender is taken up by water storage, not coal; water capacities of up to 5,000 gallons were common) and because the boiler is at pressure the water has to be forced in at an even higher pressure. This is done by the injector, which is operated by the same steam pressure that drives the locomotive. There are always two injectors and, though the working principle is the same, they take on a wide range of sizes and shapes. To add to the confusion, they are positioned in all manner of strange places around the locomotive.

Put very simply, they work by taking a jet of steam that is travelling very fast and allowing this to collect water in the form of droplets. This mixture is directed through a funnel, where its velocity is exchanged for pressure. This pressure is now higher than that of the boiler, which allows the water to push

FIG 7.7: *Basic water injector.*

Water feed

Steam

One-way valve

Feed to the boiler

Drain

open a one-way valve and enter the boiler. To know when the boiler needs water, a water-level gauge is provided in the cab and it is usually the fireman who looks after this job. For safety reasons there have to be two independent ways to check the water level, usually two water gauges, but it is permissible to have one gauge, plus a pair of 'proving' taps through which water and steam can be released. To protect the firebox should the boiler water level drop below the top, there are fuseable plugs built into the top of the copper firebox. These have a lead core that will melt if the copper is becoming too hot and are designed to release a jet of steam, not enough to douse the fire in one whoosh, but enough to create a lot of noise to attract the attention of the crew.

Before looking at the moving parts I want to finish the story of the fire by

FIG 7.8: *Glass water gauge, which permits the fireman to see when the boiler needs more water. (BRC)*

looking at the way the spent steam is used to blast the exhaust up the chimney. The basic idea is fairly simple: the exhaust steam is passed through a blast pipe and into a wide funnel facing up the chimney, which causes a partial vacuum in the smoke box and thus draws the fumes and smoke through the boiler tubes. The efficiency of these blast pipes is very important to how well a locomotive steams and several variations have been tried over the years. Many a newly-designed locomotive which steamed poorly at first has been transformed by alterations to its exhaust system.

The boiler and the firebox are insulated, fibreglass being used today, and this is then covered by a steel outer shell. It is this shell that we see beautifully painted, not the actual boiler or firebox. You will soon notice two variations in the shape of the boiler and the firebox. The Belpaire firebox has a square design that gives better water flow around the fire and improves steaming. The other, slightly more subtle, variation is the tapered boiler, where the diameter of the boiler is smaller towards the front of the locomotive. Developed by the GWR chief engineer, G. J. Churchward, it

FIG 7.9: *The forefront of locomotive design, Churchward's 1904* City of Truro, *the first locomotive in the world to break the 100 mph barrier. We can see the tapered boiler and the Belpaire square-topped firebox. The only clues to its early age are the 'old fashioned' 4-4-0 wheel arrangement and the use of double frames, that is a frame inside the driving wheels (as usual) but also a second outside frame. (GWR)*

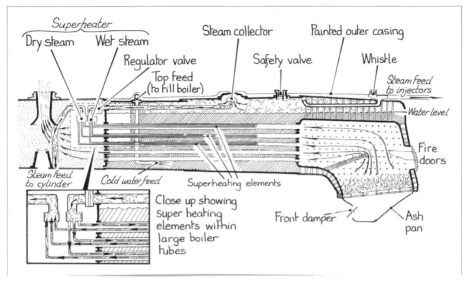

FIG 7.10: *Cross-section of a 'modern' mainline engine boiler and firebox. Note the regulator is much shallower and super-heating tubes are now in place.*

provides several useful benefits. It helps the weight distribution, it reduces the problem of the water level dropping over the firebox when going downhill and, it gives the driver better visibility looking forward. It was the design of some of the most efficient boilers ever made.

We have one last feature to explain concerning the steam. For many years, it was understood that this steam contains moisture; it is called 'saturated' steam, and will condense back to water if it is cooled. Water in the cylinders causes friction and reduces the power available. By heating the steam again, it can be transformed into a true gas; that is, all the moisture evaporates, increasing the pressure even further. This is called 'super-heated' steam and, though it is hotter still (it

can be over 400° C), it represents the absolute maximum energy that can be extracted from the fire. For many years, its use was impractical as the lubricants couldn't work at these temperatures but, by the 1920s, this problem was solved and super-heating became common on mainline locomotives. The extra heating needed is provided by taking the steam tubes back into special wide boiler tubes where the hot flue gases raise its temperature.

Now down to some work – getting the steam to drive the wheels. The steam has to be collected at the very top of the boiler and, because we don't want any water to join the steam, the collecting point is as high as possible above the water level and central, so that going up or downhill won't cause the water level to rise nearer to the take-off point. We also don't want anything that might cool the steam down; so, to keep its journey as hot as possible, the steam control valve, called the regulator, is contained within the boiler, as is the pipework to the cylinders. These pipes emerge in the smoke box and drop down to the cylinders via short insulated pipes. On later locomotives with super-heating, the regulator is often mounted in the smoke box but the 'keep it hot' principles are still maintained.

The description given at the start of this chapter of how the cylinders work was correct, but, as with the boiler, there's a bit more to it! The most important part of the process is how to admit steam to the cylinder at the right time and how to get it out at the right moment. This is the job of the valves. Originally these were slide valves, where a block with ports in it slid to and fro over apertures, which connected to each end of the cylinder. By linking the to and fro movement to the position of the cranks and thus the piston position, the necessary timing could be achieved. Slide valves, however, rely on two metal surfaces sliding one over the other – we're back to our lubrication problem with super-heated steam. To overcome this, piston valves are used instead and most restored steam engines have this type of valve to control the entry and exit of the steam.

The other important improvement that was developed from the very early locomotives was the way the steam was

FIG 7.11: *The steam chest with the piston valves in the top section and the piston and cylinder that do the work below.*

The steam feed pipe can be clearly seen dropping from the smoke box to the steam chest.

FIG 7.12: *Close-up of the cross head which supports the piston rod and keeps its motion in a straight line. The valve gear is also clear, even if a bit confusing!*

used in the cylinder. Instead of letting the steam in until the piston reached the end of the cylinder, why not let it in for a shorter time and let the expansion of that steam within the cylinder do the rest of the work to complete the piston's journey? At first the driver had just two settings: steam all the way or steam for just half the journey. Clever design of the way the valves are operated now allows the driver to control the period over which steam is admitted (called the cut-off) from almost zero right up to 100%. When the driver needs maximum power, for instance when starting a heavy train or when climbing a steep gradient, he will use a high setting, typically around 75%. This means that when the exhaust valve opens to let the used steam escape, that steam is still at virtually maximum pressure. It thus

FIG 7.13: *A valve/cylinder chest stripped down for major repairs. (GCR)*

goes up the chimney with enormous gusto and causes the great roar and high plume of steam that one sees when a locomotive starts off. As the cut-off point is reduced, the power produced is less but the efficiency is much greater because more of the steam's energy has been used to move the piston. The lower pressure of the steam at the end of the stroke also reduces the drama as it roars up the chimney and into the open air. A skilful driver and fireman team uses the appearance of the exhaust above the chimney to adjust

the way they fire and drive the loco.

Reversing a steam locomotive involves this same timing. If the steam is admitted in front of the piston, the wheel turns clockwise, but if the valves can be changed to admit it behind the piston the wheels will turn anti-clockwise.

With the exception of some experimental turbine drives in the 1920s and just one fairly successful conversion by the LMS in 1935, driving the wheels is always done by using a connecting rod and a crank. This imposes a problem on the piston rod,

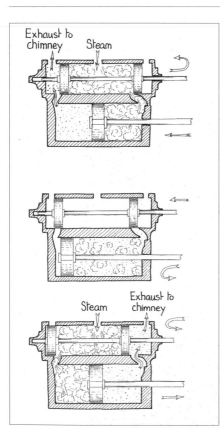

FIG 7.14: *Diagram showing the action of the valve and the piston. The valve alters the steam path to alternately push the piston forwards and then back. Here the steam is pushing the piston along the cylinder to the left.*

By moving the valve slightly it is possible to cut off the inlet port while still allowing the air and steam behind the piston to escape. The piston is now being pushed by the steam expanding within the cylinder.

Finally, the valve moves right over and the sequence begins again but now the piston is pushed to the right.

which has to move in a straight line. The piston itself holds the rod in the centre within the cylinder, and the gland through which the rod reaches the outside world is also central, but the crank causes an up and down force on the piston rod as the wheel turns. To avoid this force damaging either the rod or the gland bearing, the end of the rod is supported by one or two guide bars and the 'cross head', which absorbs the unwanted forces.

The cylinder and the cranks are usually seen on the outside of the locomotives but this is not the only position. They can be mounted between the wheels and, indeed, until the 1920s this was the more usual arrangement. By building the cranks into the axle, two cylinders can be mounted side by side beneath the smoke box, with their coupling rods driving the crank axle. These hidden 'inside' cylinders were more difficult to maintain and the valve gear had to be operated by a pair of eccentrics (clever devices that act like cranks but that can be positioned between the wheels), making the driven axle quite complex.

All combinations are in use – outside cylinders with outside valve gear, outside cylinders with inside valve gear, and inside cylinders with inside valve gear. To make this even more complex there are two, three and four-cylinder locomotives as well!

There have been several schemes for operating the valves but the two

FIG 7.15: *Close-up showing the 'extra' crank used to drive the outside valve gear. This is, in effect, bolted onto the end of the main driving crank. The square upright part of each joint is an oil reservoir.*

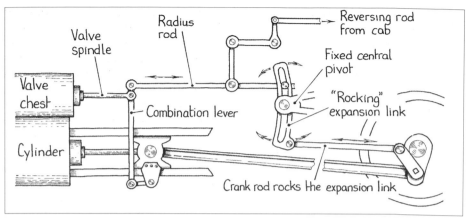

FIG 7.16: *The Walschaert's valve gear. The final movement of the valve spindle is the combination of movement from the radius rod and the combination lever. The reversing rod simply sets the position of the radius rod in the expansion link. The further from the centre it is, the further the radius rod moves and the longer the period when steam enters the cylinder.*

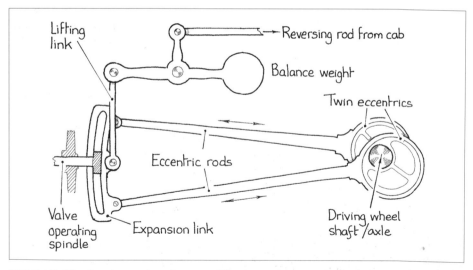

FIG 7.17: *The Stephenson's valve gear. The same expansion link idea is used but this time one end is driven approximately 90° before the crank and the other end 90° after the crank. These drives come from two eccentrics mounted on the axle. The valve spindle runs in a fixed bearing so the whole radius arm assembly is moved up and down by the reversing rod.*

standard systems are Walschaert's gear for outside valves and Stephenson's for inside valve gear.

There are two valves, one being a mirror image of the other and both moved by a common valve rod. Basically there are three events:

1. Open the exhaust valve behind the piston, and open the steam inlet valve in front of the piston.
2. Close the steam inlet valve at a point during the piston stroke as set by the driver (cut-off point).
3. To send the piston back along the cylinder this sequence is repeated but now the exhaust valve in front of the piston is opened, followed by the steam inlet valve behind the piston.

This sequence, however, is not as easy to achieve as it sounds. The changeover of the valves has to occur when the piston is turning at the start or finish of its stroke – the very point when there is relatively little movement in the piston/connecting rod/crank. To overcome this, the main valve movement is derived from its own crank, set on the main crank but at 90° to it. This movement is slightly modified by adding a small motion directly from the piston rod.

In the Stephenson's version, the valve motion is taken from two eccentrics, one set 90° before the main driving crank and the other 90° after.

If the main valve movement is reversed, then the wheels will simply be turned the other way, i.e. the engine will be in reverse.

One other rarely used variation on the cylinder arrangement is the compound engine. In this, the exhaust steam from the 'high pressure' cylinders is used to power a second low-pressure cylinder, which is coupled to the same drive shaft. The low-pressure cylinder was

FIG 7.18: *The driving axles of a locomotive, with outside cylinders and inside valve gear showing the two pairs of eccentrics which drive the radius arm. The square blocks are the bearings, which are held in slides in the main frames and allow an up and down movement of about 2 ins, controlled by heavy leaf springs. (DRC)*

FIG 7.19: *The parts you don't normally see! The boiler has been removed for repair giving us a chance to examine the frames and the inside gear. This locomotive uses inside cylinders as well as inside valve gear. The two driving cylinders are right at the top, with the valve chest between them. In the centre section we have the two connecting rods, far left and far right, with the four valve eccentric rods in the middle. At the bottom of the picture is the wheel shaft with the two driving cranks and the four eccentrics. (MHR)*

made with a larger diameter to derive as much power from the steam as possible. In locomotive design (mainly the Midland Railway) it was usual to have the high-pressure cylinders on the outside and the low-pressure compound cylinders between the axles.

When travelling at speed there is a considerable amount of weight shifting to and fro and up and down – the cranks themselves and the coupling rods all produce these forces, which are generally moving the locomotive anywhere except straight ahead. This unwanted motion can be balanced by having an equivalent mass rotating 180° from the crank, these balance weights being cast into, or bolted onto, the outside of the driving wheels.

The final problem is how to start the engine moving if both cranks happen to be at the point where the pistons are exactly at the end of the cylinder, i.e. the connecting rods are in line with the axle. This is solved by having the crank on one side of the locomotive 90° different from the other side, ensuring that one or other side will always be able to implant some rotation to the axle to get things moving. It also gives four power strokes to the driving wheels per complete revolution, providing a smoother delivery of power.

There are many other features on locomotives whose function may not be too obvious; so we'll take a stroll around a typical mainline engine and try and identify those things we can see.

Smoke deflectors were fitted each side of the smoke box on many locos and their job was to create an upward flow of air such that the smoke from

FIG 7.20: *The balance weights fitted opposite the crank pin. Note the 90° difference between the wheel nearest the camera and the far wheel. (DRC)*

FIG 7.21: *Built in 1931 at Ashford, withdrawn from British Rail service in 1964 and then stored until 1993, when a 13-year-long £120,000 restoration took place. Now immaculate, this R. Maunsell-designed Southern Railway 'U' class locomotive is back at work. Note the typical Southern Railway smoke deflector plates, low down, on each side of the smoke box. (BR)*

the chimney rose above the driving cab and prevented the driver's view from being obscured.

Sanders are a common feature situated between the driving wheels. They consist of a sand-filled box which has a feed pipe carrying the sand down close to the driving wheels. Most have a simple open or closed slide to control the flow of sand down the pipe, but some use a steam-operated jet that drives a fine stream of sand out and onto the top of the rail, where it gives the wheel much-increased grip. This is used in situations where the rail might be greasy, wet or icy and the engine is trying to start a very heavy load causing the wheels to slip. (See Fig 7.33)

Whilst near the driving wheels we will often see the pressure lubricating system. This is usually operated by a link from the valve gear and sends oil via small pipes to the various bearings. The oil used to lubricate the cylinders and valves is first mixed with steam to produce a white oil emulsion

Cylinder cocks are fitted to allow any surplus water that has accumulated in the cylinders to be driven out. This can happen when a steam engine is stationary for some time and steam has condensed in the relatively cool cylinders. If left, the first stroke of the cylinders would drive water through the valves and up the chimney, neither of which is desirable. Even worse, if the quantity of water is great, the piston may well hit the water before the exhaust valve is open so that the piston is trying to compress the water – but

FIG 7.22: *Pressure lubricating pump driven by a lever from the valve motion. (SVR)*

FIG 7.23: *Steam being blown through the cylinder drain cocks to clear any water that may have condensed in the cylinder. Note that like many GWR locomotives this uses inside valve gear, which drives the valves via cranks at the front of the steam chest. (DRC)*

FIG 7.24: *The front buffer beam, showing the train vacuum pipe, the steam heating pipe, complete with on/off tap, and a screw link coupling tied out of harm's way behind the left-hand buffer. (SVR)*

water doesn't compress! To avoid this, pressure relief valves are fitted to both ends of the cylinders.

Vacuum pipes are the way that the brakes on earlier rolling stock are controlled. The vacuum is generated on the locomotive and passed down the train via these pipes. All are provided with a blank 'parking' position, that is used to seal the last pipe in the chain.

Steam used for heating is also passed along the train by flexible pipes, though these operate at around 50 psi.

On the top of the boiler there are usually four items. From front to back these are the chimney; the steam dome covering the regulator (not always obvious); the safety valves which release steam if the boiler reaches its maximum allowed pressure; and the whistle. On some locomotives the water injection pipes are also prominent on top of the boiler.

Fig 7.26 shows three types of safety valve. The early type could be held closed to a higher pressure by adding

FIG 7.25: *This shot, taken looking down onto a class 2 mixed traffic locomotive built in 1950 to an LMS design, shows the chimney, the water injection feeds, the regulator dome and the twin 'pop' valves, one of which is releasing excess steam. The pressure oil pump and the sand box can be seen on the running plate. The two front edges of the main frames can be seen as they extend from below the boiler towards the buffer beam. (SVR)*

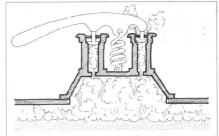

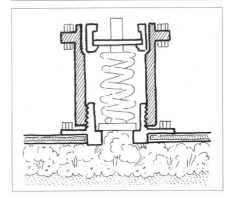

FIG 7.26: *Safety valves. Above, the early type with its easy to override lever; right top, the Ramsbottom valve with two valves and a rocking lever; and right bottom, the modern 'pop' valve.*

weights or even simply holding down the lever, the very problem that caused several boiler explosions in the early years. The Ramsbottom design overcame this, since any extra pressure applied to the lever would hold one valve closed but would raise and release the other. These valves could also be tested using the levers but, as confidence in boiler construction improved, along with more reliable pressure gauges in the cab, the non-adjustable 'pop' valve was developed. This is a reliable valve that can pass large quantities of steam, important if a large locomotive working hard has to stop unexpectedly, possibly at a signal at danger, when the fire is going to produce large amounts of steam that are no longer being used by the cylinders. The fireman cannot damp down the fire instantly and so the

FIG 7.27: *Ramsbottom valves on a South East & Chatham Railway 'P' class engine built in 1909. (KESR)*

FIG 7.28: *Possibly the prettiest tank engine of all, a C.B. Collett-designed 0-4-2, seen here working with an auto coach. (CGR)*

surplus steam must be lost. On all locomotives there must be two safety valves and on large express locomotives there are often three or four to ensure sufficient loss of steam.

Last but not least, we must note those locomotives that don't pull a separate tender – the tank engines. These usually smaller locomotives carry their water in a tank slung over the boiler (saddle tank) or in two tanks positioned on each side of the boiler (side tanks). The coal is carried in a bunker, which forms the rear of the engine. One much loved variation is the pannier tank, where the two tanks are hung along each side of the boiler but leave a clearance above the wheels.

The tank loco was also involved in a novel way of driving the train, called push-pull working, where the loco stayed coupled to one end of the coach or coaches. The driver, though, could operate either on the footplate alongside the fireman or on his own in a special driving compartment built at

FIG 7.29: *A charming saddle tank from 1897. The short wheel base allows this type of locomotive to run through very tight curves and they were usually found working in docks or large factories. (DRC)*

FIG 7.30: *A 6400 class pannier tank from 1937. The GWR panniers were made over many years in several classes but all have a similar appearance. (LR)*

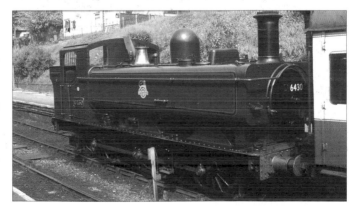

FIG 7.31: *An ex-GWR 0-6-2 tank engine (built in 1928) effortlessly hauling a five-coach train. These slightly larger tank engines were the mainstay of longer branch lines and many cross-country routes. (SR)*

the end of the last coach. This meant the unit could work either with the engine pulling the train or with it pushing. The fireman stayed on the footplate to tend the engine, regardless of the direction. Used throughout the 1930s and up to the 1950s on short branch lines, it saved time by not needing to run the engine around the train at the terminus, which also no longer needed the point work or the track for this job. There is, however, a potential problem. When pushing the coaches, they will be transmitting the power from the engine through the buffers and on curves this can mean that this force is only applied to one side of the coach. With small engines and only one or two coaches this isn't a problem but for longer trains it is. During the second half of the 20th

century, centre couplings became standard on coaching stock and this removed the off-centre problem. The idea of push-pull working was thus extended to main line services, originally between Glasgow and Edinburgh, and is now standard on many locomotive-hauled expresses, including the main London to Glasgow electric services.

Throughout the development of locomotives, there had been much experimenting on the best wheel arrangement. For sheer strength it is best to have as many powered wheels as possible touching the rails and heavy goods engines usually have four or five driven axles with relatively small diameter wheels. For speed, however, larger wheels are used and, to aid taking curves and point work at speed, a leading axle or bogie is used in front of the driving wheels. These wheels carry some of the weight of the engine and are sprung so that they can move left or right. They act as a guide to the whole engine, in effect starting the engine turning before the main rigid driving wheel group hits the curve. From the earliest times, these wheel arrangements were given a code that described the axle arrangement of the loco. The first and last figures give the number of leading and trailing wheels while the centre numbers give the number of driving wheels. For instance, a Pannier tank would be known as an 0-6-0, just having the six driving wheels, whereas a large express engine might be a 4-6-2, an arrangement known as a 'Pacific'.

I referred to the driving wheel group as being rigid but this is not strictly true. If the axles were completely rigid, then as the locomotive passed over track imperfections one or more wheels would lose contact with the rail. The ride would be pretty rough as well!

The driving axles are therefore always sprung rather like the rear wheels of a car. If you look closely at the connecting rods, you will see that there is a joint which is vital to allow the axles freedom to rise or fall over rough track. On locomotives with four or five axles, the outer axles are also mounted in special axle boxes that not only rise up and down but can also move from side to side. Again, the connecting rods have to be able to 'bend' for this to happen, in practice this is achieved by having a further vertical bearing at the connecting rod joints.

FIG 7.32: *GWR Manor class 4-6-0 showing the four-wheeled front bogie. Note the oil lamps on the buffer beam – there are four lamp brackets (three on the buffer beam and one near the top of the smoke box). One or two lamps are always carried; their position indicates the type of duty the engine is on. (SVR)*

FIG 7.33: *The left-hand joint is the wheel crank pin, that is, the point at which the to and fro motion of the coupling rod is converted into rotation of the wheel. The right-hand joint is the one that allows the wheels to have a limited vertical movement. Note also the sanders, which are used to blow sand onto the top surface of the rail to enhance grip. (GWR)*

FIG 7.34: *The top end of the tank engine range. This is a British Rail-built (1956) 2-6-4 class 4 mixed traffic locomotive, and at 88 tons this is a serious piece of machinery! (WSR)*

FIG 7.35: *For those of you who might fancy driving a steam engine, this view of the cab of a British Rail locomotive shows the relatively clean and uncluttered working area of the later 'standard' machines. This mixed traffic class 2 engine was built at Darlington in 1954. If the thrill of driving a locomotive appeals to you, many of the preserved railways offer driving experience days. (GCR)*

FIG 7.36: *Southern Railway Pacific Blackmoor Vale. The last great mainline engines with character to be produced before the standard designs of British Rail. Oliver Bulleid's 'spam cans' as they were affectionately known, were built between 1940 and 1946 to give the Southern Railway much needed, powerful mainline locomotives. They incorporated many new features, including inside valve gear that was partly driven by chains – a later source of maintenance troubles. Three classes were built: the Merchant Navy, Battle of Britain and the West Country. The latter class was lighter in weight and could be used on the SR's vast array of rural lines in Devon and Cornwall. During the late 1940s and 1950s many were rebuilt with conventional Walschaert's gear and normal cladding and worked right up to the end of steam in 1965. (BR)*

CHAPTER 8

Making it Pay

⊷ ⊱✦⊰ ⊶

Having now built our railway, equipped it with locomotives and made it safe to operate, let's look at the rolling stock.

From the very beginning, coal was the mainstay of the goods traffic. It's heavy, dirty and needs moving from mine to town or power station in vast quantities. Early coal trucks were built from wooden planks held in stout iron frames with a lift-up flap positioned in the centre of each side to enable the coal to be unloaded. The modern equivalent is much longer, made of steel and has drop-down doors in the bottom, which allow the entire contents to be dropped through the track and directly onto conveyor belts that take it to where it's needed.

For many years, these trucks were joined together by a three-link chain to convey the pull of the locomotive through the train. Stopping was controlled by sprung buffers on each

FIG 8.1: *A train of restored goods wagons. Goods vehicles have become an important part of the restoration scene in recent years. (DRC)*

FIG 8.2: *The basic three-link coupling and the triangular version. The fireman, or sometimes the cleaner, would usually couple up the train. In busy goods yards the links could be lifted on and off the hook using a hooked pole balanced across the buffer rather than by climbing in between the trucks and lifting the links by hand. (DRC)*

corner which pushed into one another to absorb the effect of slowing down. But between these two states the wagons could move freely, possibly as much as 6 ins (15 cm) to and fro between each wagon. If we imagine a train of 50 trucks, we have 24 ft (7.3m) of slack to take up! When the engine

driver applies the engine brakes, each truck will run into the one in front until the last one experiences the most awful crash. Such trains only had brakes on the engine and as these often couldn't hold the entire train on their own, a brake van, in which the poor guard travelled, was attached at the

FIG 8.3: *To eliminate the slack on passenger coaches, the screw coupling was used. Also used on goods wagons as shown here. Once the link was in place, the screw was tightened using the weighted arm (hanging down), which also made sure the coupling didn't alter during the journey. (DRC)*

FIG 8.4: *A three-link coupling between two wagons. The gap between the wagon buffers is plain to see!*

rear. His job was to apply the brake van brakes and, if he was lucky, he might not be thrown from one end of his van to the other when the train slowed down. The engine driver let the guard know when he was going to slow down by sounding a signal on the engine's whistle, which, hopefully, the guard heard.

There was one, not so obvious, benefit in having this slack between the wagons. When the locomotive started from a stationary position, the weight of each truck would be added to the load one by one as the slack was taken up. This made the job of getting the train started much easier. There was also a clever triangular-shaped link

that helped reduce the gap between wagons. By using it 'long' while lifting the chain over the hooks, it gave more room to manoeuvre, but, by then turning it so that the short side was at the top, it reduced the total distance of the coupling chain and the gap between the trucks.

A system of continuous brakes fitted to every wagon was needed and, indeed, was soon developed but most wagons, particularly coal wagons, were privately owned. The owners were none too keen to spend the money to fit such brakes and 'loose coupled' trains continued right through to the 1960s.

The same method of coupling was used for all wagons, the driving speed

FIG 8.5: *A rare example of an early wooden container sitting on a flat wagon. These containers were much too useful for general storage and very few survived into the care of the preserved railways. (SVR)*

FIG 8.6: *Two specialised tank wagons. On the left is an 'Epikote' tank, lined for oil products, and on the right a six-wheeled, glass-lined, milk wagon. (GWR)*

FIG 8.7: *Lovingly restored private owner's wagons, for general goods and the more common quarry products. This type of open six-plank truck was also used to carry vast amounts of coal. (SDR)*

FIG 8.8: *Breakdown cranes, built in a variety of sizes, were another specialist vehicle, used, hopefully rarely, to keep the railway running rather than earn revenue. This example is one of the larger ones. (PR)*

FIG 8.9: *A bogie flat wagon used to carry long loads – in this case bull-head rail in 60 ft long sections. (DRC)*

FIG 8.10: *A coach bogie showing the two side pads that steady the coach, while the weight is carried by a large centre bearing, all three covered by bricks to keep the rain out. (KESR)*

and care being the only way cattle and more fragile loads could be given a safe journey. By the 1850s the idea of a container was developed; in practice it's just an extension of packing a large box and putting it on a train. These strong wooden boxes were carried on four-wheeled flat wagons and were often collected and delivered by the railway's own lorries at each end of the journey. Steel versions emerged after the last war and by 1957 British Rail owned some 35,000 such containers. Many variations were built, including refrigerated containers for perishable goods. Today we can see long trains of the standard European size containers on almost all our main line routes.

Some of the specialised traffic may come as a surprise to us today. Explosives and munitions were regularly carried, the rules stipulating that an empty wagon should be positioned on each side whilst in

FIG 8.11: *Beautifully restored rake of Metropolitan coaches dating from 1898, photographed at work on the Bluebell Railway. (BR)*

transit. Milk was another load, for which glass-lined tanker wagons, later stainless steel, were made. Enormous quantities of milk were brought into the large cities; in 1875 the railways carried 14 million gallons a year into London alone. By the mid-1930s the total quantity topped a million gallons a day. Lorries and better organisation, introduced by the Milk Marketing Board, brought this traffic to an end in the 1980s. Oil and its by-products formed another large tanker-borne load, with each company proudly displaying its name on the sides of the tankers.

During the Second World War, long flat wagons carried tanks and even anti-aircraft guns that were fired from the train. These long bogie wagons are still used to move exceptionally heavy loads.

The need to move goods was quantified from the very beginning, indeed the driving force that created the railways had been the businesses that needed goods transported. Passengers, however, are individuals and apart from the horse-drawn coach services there was no indication of the popularity of such travel. The early lines were taken by surprise by the demand for passenger services and, indeed, the railways enabled a major change in our approach to travel. As an example, in 1851, the Great Exhibition was held in Hyde Park and Thomas Cook – yes, of travel agent fame – who was then the excursion agent for the Midland Railway, claimed to have brought some 165,000 people to London in one year, just to visit the exhibition.

Early coaches were simply stagecoaches bolted together and mounted on flat four-wheeled wagons. Second and third class passengers had

FIG 8.12: *Not a wagon, not an engine – a hand-operated truck, much beloved of old black and white films, and used for maintenance and track inspection tasks involving men and only a few tools. (KESR)*

FIG 8.13: *The idea of having an open carriage had been tried way back in the 1920s, as this Churchward-designed coach shows. Note the handle provided to aid climbing into the coach: the epitome of good design – functional and a delight to see. (SDR)*

to put up with wooden seats in open wagons! By the end of the 1800s what we would recognise as coaches were in use. These had bogies at each end and their couplings were slightly different from goods wagons, in that the chain link included a screw section that could be tightened up until the buffers touched, thus removing the notorious gap that caused so much banging on goods trains. The idea of putting the wheels in groups of four, mounted on a small truck or bogie, was evolved to enable the greater weight to be carried while permitting greater length to be achieved. Virtually all vehicles over 30 ft long, passenger or goods, employ the bogie system. The bogie is free to turn to follow the track, which, of course, immediately introduces the problem of how to operate the brakes. This is done by having the vacuum cylinders mounted under the main body of the coach. The brakes are then operated by a long, steel rod, which carries the braking action to a crank mounted under the bogie. This then operates the brakes on that bogie. The sideways movement caused by the bogie turning is minimal and the linkages are made to accommodate this.

The requirement for brakes on passenger trains had been formalised in 1889 by an Act of Parliament. It required that all the coaches should have brakes that could be applied by either the driver or the guard and, additionally, they should be auto-matically applied if the train became divided. Most lines adopted the vacuum brake system, in which a continuous brake pipe links all vehicles on the train. On the engine is a vacuum ejector, which uses a jet of steam to draw the air from the brake pipe. Some GWR engines use a mechanical pump instead. Under each coach is a pair of brake-operating cylinders, one for each bogie, which require the brake pipe to have a vacuum of around 20 inches of mercury (this equates to 10 pounds per square inch of pressure) in order to release the brakes. Thus, any reduction in the brake pipe vacuum will apply the brakes. This system means that air admitted to the brake pipe anywhere on the train will apply all the brakes – be it by the driver, the guard, or damage to the pipe.

The engines also have their own brakes, usually operated by steam pressure, though some engines use vacuum brakes. The Southern Region and London Transport adopted a steam-driven air pump which provided compressed air, stored in a reservoir, to operate the brakes.

All the brakes use a system of levers to press brake shoes onto the wheels. Only in recent times have disc brakes appeared.

The technique of having the buffers in close contact caused problems going round tight curves, as on one side the buffers would be compressed while, on the other side, the buffers wouldn't be touching. Going around reverse curves, i.e. a curve that changes direction without any straight section in between, like a letter S, always worried the operators lest the buffers should lock as the coaches changed direction. This was solved by using an American idea of a central 'solid' coupling (called a buckeye coupling) which was strong enough to convey the pushing and pulling without using the buffers at all. In practice, most coaches spent much of their life coupled together in the same order and position; so the couplings were rarely used. All modern stock uses this centre coupling system. The various other cables and pipes carrying electricity, steam for heating and brakes had to be linked across the gap dividing the coaches, as did a flexible corridor passageway which allowed staff and passengers to move between coaches. The latest modern trains still use a centre coupling that also carries all the electrical cables, braking and heating all being electrically controlled.

The other major change was the move away from individual compartments, removing some degree of privacy in exchange for a more open and accessible atmosphere. Double-glazing and air conditioning followed, providing a very pleasant journey.

FIG 8.14: *Classic preserved railway train. A 'U' class Southern Region engine hauling a five-coach train from Horsted Keynes station past the railway's stock of coaches and goods wagons. (BR)*

FIG 8.15: *Yet another special coach, an observation coach, now used regularly on steam-hauled Great Western trains in Devon. (PDR)*

Fig 8.16: *The same train en route from Paignton to Kingswear. (PDR)*

CHAPTER 9

The Romance Ends

It is undeniable that a working steam engine conveys something more than just a means of pulling trucks or coaches along a railway line. The fact that two men are using coal and water to make steam and then applying that steam to move the train gives the whole operation a 'man overcoming nature' feel. In these days of just jumping into the car, starting the engine and driving away, there is something primitive and historically interesting about steam. It is, however, a dirty, time consuming and labour-intensive way of doing the job and it would be naive to imagine that it could have continued forever. The timescale is rather odd, too. Electric traction dates back to the 1880s and diesel locomotives had been around since the 1920s; so their

FIG 9.1: *A standard class 5 locomotive, built in 1954, which like many of the BR standard locomotives had a very short working life. (NVR)*

development into reliable and efficient machines took the best part of 80 years, not exactly a rushed job!

In Britain, however, steam ended with quite peculiar haste. In 1948 the newly nationalised railways commissioned the design of nine new classes of steam locomotives – designs which covered virtually all types of traffic – surely a brave new start. In fact, within less than twelve years, the last ever steam engine had been built and the end of steam had been announced. The nostalgia and romance is enhanced by the sad way that steam passed on, culminating in dirty engines, poorly maintained. Steam was treated like some unwanted servant, nothing to do with the bright new Britain dawning in the 1960s. As ever, though, there were those who wanted to celebrate the memory of steam and preservation societies sprang up, some devoted to just buying and restoring a single locomotive, others with grander hopes of buying up and operating a complete section of closed line. The sudden and brutal closure of lines following the Beeching Report meant there was little time to act and it is to the eternal credit of the movement that so much was saved. While all countries have enthusiasts who look after earlier machines and engineering sites, Britain breeds vast numbers who devote huge amounts of time to tending our past. I am always reminded of the Lynton and Barnstable railway in Devon. This charming narrow gauge line plied its business from 1898 to 1935, just 37 years, yet it has an enormous following of people, almost none of whom ever saw it working! The first book written to record its life was published in 1936 and was still selling in the 1960s. Today, there are more books in print about this line than ever before and even a short section has been rebuilt and runs trains. Who says nostalgia isn't what it used to be?

With the demise of steam locomotives came the end of the vast array of facilities that were needed to tend these machines. Though in engineering terms the steam engine is fairly basic compared to the diesel or electric version, it had always needed great attention. The obvious ritual of lighting the fire, getting the steam up to pressure and then cleaning it all at the start of the day was only part of the story. Steam locomotives need water, lots of water. Almost every large station would have water columns at the ends of the platforms where the tender could be refilled during a short stop. On main lines troughs were built between the lines and filled with water. Fitted to the tender would be a scoop that could be lowered into these troughs, which, as the train was moving forward, sent a column of water up a large pipe and into the water tank in the tender. This was essential for all long-distance, non-stop trains and was used on all lines except the Southern Region, which still relied on stopping at major towns en route. Water corrodes the copper of the firebox and the steel of the boiler and, in most large depots, the water supply was taken through a water softening plant, as it is today on many of the preserved lines.

Not all coal burns the same way and

FIG 9.2: *An unusual view of a tender with the front removed. Only the centre section holds coal; all the rest is for water. Capacities up to 5,000 gallons were common. (NYMR)*

FIG 9.3: *Inside a fairly large engine shed, showing the pits beneath the locos for inspection and maintenance. Note the smoke hoods above the chimneys to extract smoke. (DRC)*

the type and quality of the coal was very important. Like the water, coal had to be stored, it had to be transported and it had to be delivered into the tender. All this meant buildings, machinery and space. Ash pits, where the fire was 'dropped' during cleaning, were needed, as were pits to enable the cylinders, valve gear and axles situated between the wheels to be inspected and lubricated. Some of this work was simplified in the later BR standard locomotives by using pressure-driven central oiling systems and having much better access to the moving parts, but the vast infrastructure of the steam days had to be there.

Just compare this to the needs of the diesel or electric locos. Diesel requires storage tanks and a garage-like means of filling the tanks. By volume and weight, diesel fuel is vastly more efficient than coal and water. No water tanks or water columns, no turntables to turn a tender locomotive around for its return journey. No corrosion problems, and in the frosts of winter, a

FIG 9.4: *Taking water from a platform water column. Note the drip funnel where the hose normally rests. The stop valve is mounted below the platform level and is operated by a handle. (SVR)*

simple electric heater will keep a diesel engine safe compared to the problem of keeping a steam engine and tender ice-free. If you see a new industrial estate or shopping development near a railway station, it's a fair bet that it has been built on the site of the old goods yards, engine sheds and sidings. Nevertheless, all of today's steam railways have to have at least a version of these early facilities.

Meanwhile, what of our national railway network? The trains themselves have steadily evolved. The High Speed Train (HST), designed to reach 125 mph and introduced in 1976, set several speed records and was scheduled to cover the London to Bristol run *averaging* over 90 mph. The diesel speed record soon climbed to over 160 mph. The unfortunate tilting train (APT) reached a British record speed of 162 mph on a trial run in 1979. In 1991 a special press journey in the then new

FIG 9.5: *A coaling plant. The coal trucks are hauled up to the loading floor (dark arch on the left), where the coal is loaded into small wagons which can be tipped to drop it down chutes and into the awaiting tender on the lower line. Nearer the camera is the pit used to collect the ash when the locomotive's fire is 'dropped' at the end of the day. The building is also used to support a vast water tank which feeds all the water columns around the works. (DRC)*

FIG 9.6: *A bygone sight, a turntable, essential to turn express steam locomotives round at the end of their journeys. (DRC)*

electric Intercity 225s managed a superb run from London to Edinburgh in 3½ hours, averaging 112 mph. Despite some very fast trains elsewhere in the world, Britain runs more trains scheduled to travel at over 100 mph than any other country in Europe.

Long the butt of jokes, our railways have quietly lurched into a position where the service is probably better than ever: most lines are running with high passenger figures and the latest trains are quiet, fast and comfortable.

An interesting bridge between the preserved lines and modern day trains is the running of steam 'specials' over normal main lines. Over a hundred such journeys take place every year.

FIG 9.7: *The HST, the first widely used modern train in Britain. The powerful units with six or seven coaches between two locomotives still provide many long-distance services 30 years after they first appeared.*

FIG 9.8: *The modern HST replacement, built in both electric and diesel versions, providing a very pleasant ride. Designed and built by the French-Canadian Bombardier company.*

FIG 9.9: *The end of an era, or perhaps the inspiration for generations to come. (LR)*

SECTION IV

REFERENCE

A selection of museums and working steam railways is listed below, all of which would make a fascinating day out for the whole family. Children are more than welcome at preserved railway sites (Thomas the Tank Engine events are regularly held) but remember steam engines are hot, oily and will often make a lot of noise – if a steam safety valve lifts, the noise is very loud. I recently saw a young girl who had shown interest up to the moment the engine released steam, but sadly she left in tears, frightened and definitely not anxious to come back! Incidentally, the engine crew don't know when a safety valve may lift, so they can't warn you.

Dirt or at least coal dust is the other thing to be aware of, so don't bring the kids in their Sunday best. It is usually possible to walk a dog with you on a lead but, again, beware noises that may frighten it. Though most train movements are slow (there is a general speed limit of 25 mph on restored railways), do take extra care if your children haven't seen a steam railway before.

Most sites have toilets, refreshment facilities, a shop and provision for wheelchairs. Some of the larger ones have full restaurant facilities, including dining trains, which make a very nice change for celebrating a special event, even if the party aren't all railway fans. (Dining trains always need booking in advance.)

All the sites mentioned have a website, generally very good and giving details of opening times and the cost of tickets. They also show special events, which are very popular.

There are several railway-related magazines but two specialise in the preserved railway scene, *Steam Railway* and *Heritage Railway*, both usually available in WH Smith's.

Lastly, please remember almost everything you see and touch has been lovingly restored, often from complete wrecks, involving hundreds and hundreds of hours of skilled work.

Enjoy.

The following is a selection of standard gauge lines, many open outside the main season, for bank holidays, half-term periods and special events, but, as timetables change, I have omitted opening times. Instead I suggest you check the websites or telephone before travelling any distance.

An asterisk indicates a site which has steam-hauled passenger trains operating over a route of at least one mile. The initials t/t indicate a telephone timetable.

NORTH WEST

CARNFORTH STATION & VISITORS CENTRE, Carnforth. www.carnforth-station.co.uk	01524 735165
*EAST LANCASHIRE RAILWAY, Bury. www.east-lancs-rly.co.uk	0161 764 7790
*EMBSAY & BOLTON ABBEY STEAM RAILWAY, Embsay, nr Skipton. www.embsayboltonabbeyrailway.org.uk	01756 10614 (t/t 01756 795189)
*LAKESIDE & HAVERTHWAITE RAILWAY, nr Ulverston. www.lakesiderailway.co.uk	01539 531594
MUSEUM OF SCIENCE & INDUSTRY, Manchester. www.msim.org.uk	0161 832 2244
*RIBBLE STEAM RAILWAY, Preston. www.ribblesteam.org.uk	01772 728800

NORTH EAST

BEAMISH OPEN AIR MUSEUM. Beamish, Co. Durham. www.beamish.org.uk.	0191 370 4000
BOWES RAILWAY, Gateshead. www.bowesrailway.co.uk	0191 416 1847
DARLINGTON RAILWAY CENTRE & MUSEUM, Darlington. www.drcm.org.uk.	01325 460532
ELSECAR RAILWAY PRESERVATION GROUP www.barnsley.gov.uk/leisure/elsecar	01226 746746
INGROW LOCO MUSEUM, Ingrow Station. www.bahamas45596.co.uk	01535 690739
*KEIGHLEY & WORTH VALLEY RAILWAY, Keighley. www.kwvr.co.uk	01535 645214 (t/t 01535 64777)
LEEDS INDUSTRIAL MUSEUM, Armley Mills. www.leeds.gov. uk/armleymills	01132 637861
LOCOMOTION: THE NATIONAL RAILWAY MUSEUM AT SHILDON, Shildon. www.locomotion.uk.com	01388 777999
MIDDLETON RAILWAY, Leeds. www.middletonrailway.org.uk	0113 270320
NATIONAL RAILWAY MUSEUM, York. The World's Largest Railway Museum. www.nrm.org.uk	01904 621261
*NORTH YORKSHIRE MOORS RAILWAY, Pickering. www.northyorkshiremoorsrailway.com	01751 472508

*TANFIELD RAILWAY, Gateshead.   0191 388 7545
www.tanfield-railway.co.uk
VINTAGE CARRIAGES TRUST, Ingrow, Keighley. 01535 680425
www.vintagecarriagestrust.org

WALES
GRIFFITHS TOWN RAILWAY MUSEUM, Pontypool. 01495 762908
GWILI RAILWAY, Bronwydd Arms, Carmarthen. 01267 230666
www.gwili-railway.co.uk
*LLANGOLLEN RAILWAY, Llangollen. 01978 860979
www.llangollen-railway.co.uk   (t/t 01978 860951)
SWANSEA VALE RAILWAY, Llansamlet. 01792 461000

WEST MIDLANDS
*CHASEWATER RAILWAY, Brownhills West. 01543 452623
www.chaserail.com
*CHURNET VALLEY RAILWAY, Cheddleton, nr Leek. 08707 666312
www.churnet-valley-railway.co.uk
*FOXFIELD STEAM RAILWAY, Blythe Bridge, Stoke-on-Trent. 01782 396210
www.foxfieldrailway.co.uk
*GLOUCESTERSHIRE WARWICKSHIRE RAILWAY, Toddington. 01242 621405
www.gwsr.com
IRONBRIDGE GORGE MUSEUM, Telford. 01952 432166
www.ironbridgegorge.org.uk
*SEVERN VALLEY RAILWAY, Bewdley. 01299 403816
www.svr.co.uk

EAST MIDLANDS
APPLEBY-FRODINGHAM RAILWAY PRESERVATION SOCIETY, 01652 656661
Brigg. www.afrps.co.uk
BARROW HILL ROUNDHOUSE MUSEUM, Staveley. 01246 472450
www.barrowhill.org.uk
*BATTLEFIELD LINE, Shackerstone. 01827 880754
www.battlefield-line-railway.co.uk
*CRICH TRAMWAY VILLAGE, Matlock. 01773 854321
www.tramway.co.uk
*GREAT CENTRAL RAILWAY, Loughborough. 01509 230726
www.gcrailway.co.uk   (t/t 01509 211599)
*ECCLESBOURNE RAILWAY, Winksworth, Derbyshire.
www.wyvernrail.co.uk
LINCOLNSHIRE WOLDS RAILWAY, Ludborough. 01507 363881
www.lincolnshirewoldsrailway. co.uk
*MIDLAND RAILWAY – BUTTERLEY, Ripley. 01773 570140
www.midlandrailwaycentre.co.uk
*NENE VALLEY RAILWAY, Peterborough. 01780 784444
www.nvr.org.uk   (t/t 01780 78440)

*NORTHAMPTON & LAMPORT RAILWAY, Chapel Brampton.   01604 820327
www.nlr.org.uk
NORTHAMPTON IRONSTONE RAILWAY TRUST, Northampton.   01604 702031
*PEAK RAIL, Matlock. www.peakrail.co.uk   (t/t 01629 580381)
RUTLAND RAILWAY MUSEUM, Cottesmore.   01572 813203
SNIBSTON DISCOVERY PARK, Coalville.   01530 278444
www.leics. gov.uk/museums

EAST ANGLIA
*BRESSINGHAM STEAM MUSEUM, Bressingham, nr Diss.   01379 686900
www.bressingham. co.uk
EAST ANGLIAN RAILWAY MUSEUM, nr Colchester.   01206 242524
www.earm.co.uk
MANGAPPS RAILWAY & MUSEUM, Burnham-on-Crouch.   01621 784898
www.mangapps. co.uk
*MID-NORFOLK RAILWAY, Dereham.   01362 690633
www.mnr.org.uk
*NORTH NORFOLK RAILWAY, Sheringham.   01263 820800
www.nnr.co.uk   (t/t 01263 820800)

SOUTH WEST
*AVON VALLEY RAILWAY, Bitton, Bristol.   0117 932 5538
www. avonvalleyrailway.co.uk   (t/t 0117 932 7296)
*BODMIN & WENFORD RAILWAY, Bodmin.   01208 73666
www.bodminandwenfordrailway.co.uk
BRISTOL HARBOUR RAILWAY & INDUSTRIAL MUSEUM, Bristol. 0117 9031570
DARTMOOR RAILWAY, Okehampton. www.dartmoorrailway.co.uk   01837 55667
*DEAN FOREST RAILWAY, Norchard, Lydney.   01594 845840
www.deanforestrailway. co.uk   (t/t 01594 843423)
*EAST SOMERSET RAILWAY, Cranmore.   01749 880417
www.eastsomersetrailway.com
*ISLE OF WIGHT STEAM RAILWAY, Havenstreet.   01983 882204
www. iwsteamrailway.co.uk   (t/t 01983 884343)
*PAIGNTON & DARTMOUTH STEAM RAILWAY, Devon.   01803 555872
SOMERSET & DORSET RAILWAY TRUST, Washford Station, 01984 640869
West Somerset Railway. www.sdrt.org.uk
*SOUTH DEVON RAILWAY, Buckfastleigh.   01364 642338
www. southdevonrailway.org
STEAM – MUSEUM OF THE GREAT WESTERN RAILWAY,   01793 466646
Swindon. www.swindon.gov.uk/steam
*SWANAGE RAILWAY, Swanage.   01929 425800
www.swanagerailway.co.uk
*SWINDON & CRICKLADE RAILWAY, Blunsdon Station, Swindon. 01793 771615
www.swindon-cricklade-railway.org
*WEST SOMERSET RAILWAY, Minehead.   01643 704996
www.west-somerset-railway.co.uk

YEOVIL RAILWAY CENTRE, Stoford, nr Yeovil.   01935 410420
www.yeovilrailway.freeservers.com

LONDON & SOUTH EAST

*BLUEBELL RAILWAY, Sheffield Park, E. Sussex.   01825 720800
www.bluebell-railway.co.uk
BUCKINGHAMSHIRE RAILWAY CENTRE, Quainton Road, Bucks.   01296 655450
www.bucksrailcentre.org
*CHINNOR & PRINCES RISBOROUGH RAILWAY, Chinnor.   01844 354117
www.cprra.co.uk   (t/t 01844 353535)
CHOLSEY & WALLINGFORD RAILWAY, Oxon.   01491 835067
wwwcholsey-wallingford-railway.com
COLNE VALLEY RAILWAY, Halstead, Essex.   01787 461174
www.colnevalleyrailway.co.uk
DIDCOT RAILWAY CENTRE, Didcot.   01235 817200
www.didcotrailwaycentre.org.uk
*EAST KENT RAILWAY, Shepherdswell.   01304 832042
www.eastkentrailway.com
*EPPING ONGAR RAILWAY, Ongar.   01277 366616
www.eorailway.co.uk
*KENT & EAST SUSSEX RAILWAY, Tenterden.   01580 765155
www.kesr.org.uk
LAVENDER LINE, Isfield, nr Uckfield.   01825 750515
www.lavender-line.co.uk
*MID-HANTS RAILWAY, Alresford.   01962 733810
www.watercressline.co.uk.   (t/t 01962 734866)
NORTH WOOLWICH OLD STATION MUSEUM,   020 7474 7244
North Woolwich, E16. www.newham.gov.uk
SPA VALLEY RAILWAY, Tunbridge Wells.   01892 537715
www.spavalleyrailway.co.uk

Narrow Gauge Lines

It would be most unfair not to mention five gallant narrow gauge lines, all in Wales.
Two were built in the 19th century to convey slate, the other three, early in the
20th century, as tourist lines. All have been fully restored and now carry passengers.

*FFESTINIOG RAILWAY, Porthmadoc.   01766 516000
Possibly the best known of our narrow gauge lines. www.festrail.co.uk
*WELSH HIGHLAND RAILWAY, Caernarfon. Currently operating over some twelve
miles of track, the eventual aim is to restore the line right through to Porthmadoc.
Contact details as per the Ffestiniog.
*TALYLLYN RAILWAY, Tywyn.   01654 710472
The first railway in the country to be restored by enthusiasts. www.talyllyn.co.uk
*VALE OF RHEIDOL RAILWAY, Aberystwyth.   01970 625819
Once British Rail's only narrow gauge line. wwwrheidolrailway.co.uk
*WELSHPOOL & LLANFAIR LIGHT RAILWAY,   01938 810441
Llanfair Caereinion. www.wllr.org.uk

GLOSSARY

BALLAST	Stones used as a bed for railway track.
BLAST PIPE	A cone-shaped pipe through which used steam is driven in order to draw smoke through the boiler.
BLOCK	A section of track on which only one train is allowed.
BOGIE	An assembly of axles, usually two, which are free to turn as a single unit.
BRAKE VAN	A special covered goods wagon provided with hand-operated brakes.
BROAD GAUGE	A track system with the rails spaced 7 ft ¼ in apart.
BUFFERS	Devices to absorb the impact of two trucks or coaches bumping into each other.
CAB	Area of a locomotive where the driver and fireman work.
CATTLE DOCK	A raised and enclosed area at stations where cattle could be loaded onto and from wagons.
CHAIRS	Devices fixed to the sleepers that hold the rail in place.
COUPLING	A device for joining wagons or coaches together.
CROSS HEAD	Part of the guiding system used to join the piston to the driving wheels on a locomotive.
CUT-OFF	The proportion of the piston stroke that receives steam.
CUTTING	A channel cut through the ground to enable the track to pass through a hill.
CYLINDER	A tube that contains the piston.
ECCENTRIC	A form of crank that doesn't need to interrupt the axle.
EDGE RAIL	A rail where the wheels run along the top edge.
EJECTOR	A steam-operated device that creates a vacuum.
EMBANKMENT	An earthwork that raises the railway in order to cross a valley.
FIREBOX	The enclosed box which houses the fire in a locomotive.
FISHPLATE	A metal bar used to join sections of rail together.
FLANGE	A projection around the rim of a wheel.
FRAME	The basic chassis of a locomotive.
FROG	The section of a point that allows the wheels to cross through a gap in a rail.
GAUGE	The distance between the inside edges of the two rails.
GROUND SIGNAL	A small round signal placed at ground level, used for shunting.
INCLINE	A section of track too steep for a locomotive to climb.
INJECTOR	A steam-operated device for pumping water into the boiler on a locomotive.

INTERLOCKING	A mechanism to prevent incorrect or dangerous setting of signals and pointwork.
LIGHT RAILWAY	A railway constructed to carry less weight than a standard line but restricted to 25 mph speeds.
LOADING BAY	A raised area level with the floor of a wagon to allow easy loading or unloading of goods.
NARROW GAUGE	A track gauge less than the standard 4 ft 8½ ins.
PISTON	A disc which fits inside a cylinder.
PULLMAN	A type of luxurious passenger coach designed by the American Pullman Company.
RAILCAR	A single self-contained coach which includes an engine.
REGULATOR	A device to control the flow of steam from the boiler.
SAFETY VALVE	A device that will release steam if the boiler pressure becomes too high.
SEMAPHORE	A signal that uses an arm which is raised or lowered.
SHUNTER	A small locomotive designed for moving trucks and coaches short distances.
SIGNAL BOX	A raised building in which the signalman can control the points and signals in his area.
SLEEPER	A wooden, steel or concrete beam used to hold the rails.
SMOKEBOX	The area at the front of the boiler where the smoke is collected before being driven up the chimney.
SMOKE TUBES	Pipes that carry the smoke from the fire through the boiler.
STAY	A type of bolt used to hold the inner firebox within the boiler.
STEAM BLOWER	A device to inject a blast of steam up the chimney to draw the fire when the locomotive is stationary.
SUPER-HEATING	Increasing the temperature of conventional steam vapour.
TANK ENGINE	A locomotive that carries its own coal and water.
TELEGRAPH	An early electrical system for sending messages.
TENDER	A special wagon pulled by a locomotive that carries the coal and water.
TOKEN	A type of key used in the signal equipment to ensure that only one train is in a section of single line track.
TRAM PLATEWAY	An L-shaped rail where the wheels run on the bottom surface.
VACUUM BRAKING	A type of braking system that uses a vacuum to release the brakes.
VALVE	A device that controls the flow of steam.
WATER GAUGE	A device that allows the fireman to see the water level in the boiler.

INDEX

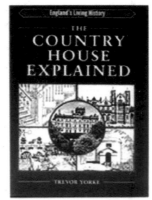

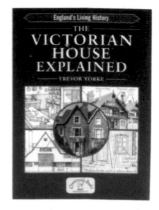

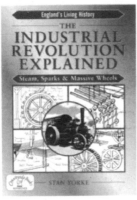

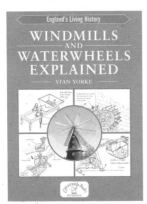

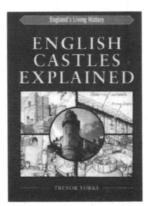

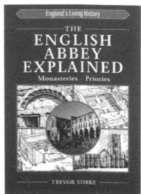